GASLIGHTING & NARCISSISTIC ABUSE RECOVERY

RECOVER FROM EMOTIONAL ABUSE, RECOGNIZE
NARCISSISTS & MANIPULATORS AND BREAK FREE
ONCE AND FOR ALL

DON BARLOW

A ROADTOTRANQUILITY BOOK

CONTENTS

Before we get into the book, let me offer you a free mini-book. Scan this QR code to claim your FREE People-Pleasing No More mini-book!

INTRODUCTION

When I was four years old, I loved preschool. For the first time in my young life, I could stand up and share something about myself without my teacher or classmates rolling their eyes in response to my enthusiasm.

"This is my new truck," I told them one time. "I love it because it rolls really fast and it's a nice blue."

I stared in awe as they leaned forward, nodded in agreement. It was definitely a nice blue.

Then I went home, and everything changed. There, if I wanted to talk about myself, I had to pay the price.

Mom made sure to trip over my beloved truck, despite how I'd deliberately placed it well out of her way. I knew better than to play in the living room or kitchen.

"Why is this here!?" she'd roar. I would try to tell her it was next to the toy box—which was where I played—but my answer would always be stomped on... like so many of my other beloved toys.

"I don't want to hear your ridiculous excuses! I could have broken my neck." Then she'd stomp off to the kitchen, pour herself another cup of coffee, and talk on the phone for the rest of the day. As far as she was concerned, our minor tiff was all the parenting I required as a child.

Whenever I lived these moments, they ripped my heart out. It seemed that no matter how hard I tried to be good—to play quietly and earn praise—all I ended up doing instead was causing trouble.

My presence seemed to put my mother on edge, and rather than defend his son, my father would always side with my mother, leaning into her dramatics as if her opinion mattered far more than my development.

All of this fighting and stress made me develop ulcers at ten and acid reflux at 13, and it also inspired me to run away at 17. It wasn't until my parents stopped taking up all the space in my life that I could finally take a moment to breathe.

Their constant pressure and demands felt so normal to me at the time though that once I got away from them, it was like landing on another planet. Suddenly, I could take up space, say what I wanted, forget to wash a dish, and even express an opinion. Those first few weeks on my own gave me so much freedom that I nearly fainted from happiness.

I chose to study psychology in school. I'd always loved my classes, but after years of assurance from Mom and Dad that I wasn't "college material," it took a big mental leap to walk through the double doors of the university. However, I managed to push, and they opened to a wonderful world where people and their actions came with a science behind them.

I spent five years studying the logic behind emotional manipulation, verbal abuse, and their effects on our wellbeing and ability to have healthy relationships. I also learned the proper term for people like my mom and dad: *narcissists*.

During my studies, I met and dated several lovely young women. However, I noticed something odd—I seemed drawn to women who made me doubt what I knew to be true. All of my exes seemed to follow a script; I would meet them and feel enchanted by how they laughed or tossed their hair, their extreme intelligence, and how they had a clear passion for their chosen fields.

Then, I'd spend some time with them and hear an off-hand comment made about someone else, but only in private. One of my partners confided that she "wished that her professor had her [my partner's] brains," which I found strange. The class she referred to was a lecture packed with hundreds of undergrads; it would have been a shock if her professor knew her name at all.

It went downhill from there. Fights over what I thought were simple misunderstandings or miscommunications would escalate into accusations of "you never loved me!" or something on that level. It would be up to me to grovel and beg for forgiveness, which was doled out in the smallest pieces you can imagine.

Finally, a female friend of mine named Connie pulled me aside one day for a coffee. We got into one of those deep, hours-long conversations that is so easy to have on a college campus.

"Listen, you need to reconcile your patterns. You're dating your mother over and over again," she told me.

"What?" I countered, the blood draining from my face. "How can you say that?"

She shrugged. "Hey, it's what you know. It's how you were raised. When you see that spark of narcissism in a woman, you run right to her. Trust me, I've seen you do it." She took a long drink from her latte as I stared at her. "We all do it; we stick to what's familiar to us. When that happens, we have to break down our habits so we can leave them behind. It's the only way to move forward."

I left Connie that evening with my heart pounding. Was she right? Was I stuck in a loop of bad relationships because some sick part of me *wanted* them?

That conversation changed my life. It inspired me to write my dissertation on dating patterns and their parallels to our parents. A large group of incredible people offered to let me interview them and dig deeper into how they dated and fell in love. The experience opened my understanding up in ways I never imagined.

To me, everyone's patterns seemed crystal clear. Student X was raised by Parent Y who had a specific personality, and then Student X would go on to date others with the same traits as Parent Y. Yet, the people I interviewed disagreed with me whenever I pointed out that fact. They'd insist that their last relationship was a left turn from their norm; there were other reasons it didn't work out.

The saddest moment of my study came when I saw how few people who dated narcissists realized they were in a highly manipulative relationship. They described their partners as "really funny" or "so smart," despite how bad they felt in that person's company.

After I graduated, I kept in touch with many of those same people who helped me get my Masters. Most of them eventually got married, and many of those who were partners to hardened narcissists got divorced. It wasn't until the dust settled on their messy legal battles and screaming matches in the front yard that they finally looked themselves in the mirror and asked, "what was I thinking?"

Manipulative relationships are impossible to see from the inside, yet when we find ourselves in one, we can still sense that something is wrong. Every time we try to pin down what exactly could be the issue, we're quickly assured by our partner that we're way off. This could be thanks to a sudden rush of sweetness or a big fight in which we find ourselves apologizing, though we're not quite sure why we're the sorry ones.

That's why I decided to write this book. I wanted to help people who got lost in that bad relationship fog that makes love impossible to navigate. Healthy relationships are a constant give and take—a kind of cooperative dance. However, unhealthy relationships can disguise themselves as passion, drama, and even a state of balance. It's only with the right vocabulary and mental tools that we can escape the illusion and see the truth: that we're being used to feed our partner's ego.

I approached this book with hope for anyone feeling a low self-esteem, loss of who they are, or inability to express themselves or grow as a person from being part of a bad relationship. As someone who felt caught in the same trap many times myself, I come from a place of empathy and understanding. These situations are no one's fault, and we always have a way out. No one is trapped or obligated to stay in a destructive relationship.

To help you get away from the person claiming to love you while they slowly destroy you, I outline several ways to recognize toxic behavior and how to respond to it. I also look into the psychology behind narcissism, gaslighting tactics, and why some people feel the need to do these things, even though it doesn't benefit them in the long run. Then, we'll get into how you can care for yourself, create a safe space for yourself, and why you must prioritize your mental health.

It's my goal to get you to a mental space that feels confident and sure enough to help you walk away from a bad partner—not fix or change anyone. No one needs fixing; we all need to live a life that makes us happy and confident. I'm guessing that if you picked up this book, you're not feeling either of those things right now. Don't worry, you will, but you have to do the work.

I've worked with hundreds of people who felt tied to someone or stuck in a rut that kept them from entering a good, balanced relationship. Each of us is unique and has our own needs, but I've found that there are some fundamental things a victim of narcissism can do to better their life. I want to share these tactics with you and help you move forward. You deserve happiness and love.

This book will help you understand your partner and yourself better, identify the problem you are having, and what you need to be happy. It will also help you stand up to whoever is making you feel devalued. Are you ready to leave but can't seem to make yourself stand up and walk out the door? I'm here to help.

Spare yourself the long-term hate and negativity that can fester if you choose to ignore the problem and stay in this relationship. It won't get better and your partner will not change. You can change, but you have to decide that you're ready and willing to do something different. Maybe the narcissist in your life isn't someone you can break up with —it could be a parent, sibling, or even a boss. Maybe it's your nearest and dearest friend. Whoever is making you question your worth, it's time to turn the tables and feel amazing about your talents, your character, and what you contribute to the world.

Narcissists win when we feel small. It's time for you and your self-worth to fill up the universe.

Keep reading to learn more about how you can change your situation. Today is your day.

You deserve it.

1

THE NARCISSIST'S PLAYBOOK

Let's start off with a simple question: what is a narcissist?

Narcissism is a personality. A narcissist exhibits traits that send a singular message: "I come first." This person might manipulate those around them, tell lies, deny saying or doing anything that could cause potential embarrassment, or be abusive.

It also occurs on a spectrum. That means you might recognize certain narcissistic traits in many people but only see extreme examples here and there. Self-assurance and a high confidence can help us as we go through life. We can get more jobs if we appear put together and sure of ourselves. Confident teachers can influence their students to pay closer attention in class and score higher on tests. A little narcissism can go a long way.

Traits like self-assurance and self-admiration can easily get out of control. I'm certain you've met a narcissist many times yourself and saw it right away.

Maybe someone at a party wanted to be your best friend one minute, and then seemed to forget you the moment someone who seemed "better" came along. Perhaps you've had someone offer to help you out with a project, only to conveniently forget about it the day you're scheduled to meet. You might have a coworker who takes credit for others' ideas or whom you know better than to trust.

Psychologists characterize narcissism by their grandiose sense of self-importance, a lack of caring or empathy for others, need for endless admiration, and a belief that they hold some special place in the world and should be recognized as a unique and beautiful creature.

A grandiose sense of self doesn't sound terrible on the surface, but it can manifest in ways we don't expect. I can give my own personal example—a couple friends of mine from university kept in touch with a guy named Scott they studied with in forestry class. The three of them lived in different states but kept in touch using an online group chat, all making sure to check in on each other from time to time.

Without warning, Scott dumped his two friends. He sat down and wrote them each a long, formal letter to inform them that he would no longer allow them to hold him back. They'd done enough damage, and he planned to move on. Scott asked them not to contact or attempt to make up with him. He couldn't handle them and their toxic energy anymore.

My two friends told me this story with smiles on their faces, though the circumstances disturbed me deeply. I'd known Scott in school, but we never had classes together. Instead, I'd see him at parties, pulling out his poetry and insisting everyone listen while he read one out loud. I made the mistake of listening to a piece so bad I audibly groaned. Everyone looked at me like I was insane, but hey—that poem stank.

So, Scott dumped two old school friends. Who cares? Well, I did. I saw some disturbing stuff in his decision to write those letters.

First, the three of them weren't close. They only got together for a beer a few times a year, and they jumped on a video conference even less often. This was a low-stakes relationship that no one lost sleep over.

Second, there was no need for a letter. All Scott had to do was politely turn down the next invitation he received to meet his friends. We've all done it—we find some flimsy excuse to sit at home and binge a show instead of braving the outside world. Why was Scott unable to find some excuse to sit out the next round of drinks?

Finally, the wording of the letters spoke volumes about Scott's worldview. He mentioned that his "time was valuable" and he couldn't "bend to the will of others" anymore. He seemed to think that he needed to take a stand and assert himself with two people who didn't need anything like this from him if he wanted to part ways.

Scott's behavior aligns perfectly with a test created by Robert Raskin and Calvin S. Hall back in the late seventies. It is known as the Narcissistic Personality Inventory (NPI). I can almost hear Scott saying some of the phrases present on the test.

"I find it easy to manipulate people."

"I usually get the respect that I deserve."

That letter was Scott's NPI, and he scored off the charts.

We should be able to spot a narcissist a mile away, right? Not necessarily. Narcissists never lead with the bad stuff; rather, they pull us in by lavishing us with attention and compliments. They offer a fun, edgy friendship or an opportunity to try something new. They tell us they feel connected to us more than they do to anyone else.

Narcissism can be anywhere from mild to out of control. You likely know someone who's generally a great person but does one or two things that boggle or bother you.

Connie, my truth-telling friend from the introduction, had a girl-friend who needed everyone to tell her she was intelligent. If she didn't hear it on a regular basis, she'd start quoting literature or casually dropping into casual conversation how she spoke four languages. Whenever someone was taken aback by her knowledge of ancient history and commented on how smart she was, this friend glowed.

It made her day.

Sure, it drove Connie bonkers that her friend needed so much positive reinforcement. They even fought about it a few times when Connie felt her friend crossed a line, making others feel dumb so they'd see her as mentally superior. However, for the most part, they still stayed friends.

"I know it's a narcissistic trait," she admitted to me once, "but the same narcissism makes her a fun friend. There's no one else I'd rather have on my side in a debate or hang out with at a party."

Now, Connie made sure not to bring this girl to her wedding party when she married her partner, but she was still among the guests.

I like to think of lower-level narcissists this way—be honest with yourself and don't make them a best man or maid-of-honor. But hey, you can still invite them to the wedding. They'll always jump up and dance.

That same level of fun and excitement makes narcissists easy to forgive and hard to spot, particularly when we choose them as partners. They almost completely blur our vision once we get too close. It's not until we've spent a long time by their side that our view will begin to sharpen. Sometimes that clear, unhindered view shows us that we've made a terrible mistake.

Narcissists at the high end of the spectrum can have a disorder known as Narcissistic Personality Disorder, (NPD). It is a personality disorder, meaning that it is a mentality that keeps the person from functioning normally. About one in 2000 people have it, and the majority identify as males; however, women can still have it, (I know better than anyone they absolutely can), it's just less common.

Think back to some of the coworkers you had in your current or past job. Do you remember anyone who seemed so charming and witty in a meeting, but also got completely put off when asked to do something menial like making copies? Maybe this person got disgusted if anyone interrupted them, even if it was an accident. You probably saw them get incredibly angry because they had to turn in a standard form that they forgot and railed about it for hours.

I hear tons of stories about people whom I suspect are clear cases of NPD. These people rarely get fired from their jobs. They stomp out with their heads thrown back and the doors wide open, so the whole world can see that your boss just made a big mistake.

That need for tension, drama, and attention keep those with NPD from living a normal life. Friendships become tests to see if the other party is devoted enough—can grovel hard enough—for the NPD's approval. Every job interview is a farce—everyone knows that the one with NPD is the smartest person in the building, and this company would be lucky to have them.

This obsession with themselves drives friends, family, and opportunities away regularly. Who can blame anyone for walking away from a person who finds their own reflection to be the most interesting person in the room?

The sad thing is that these people have a mental illness. NPD is one of ten personality disorders, and its nature makes those who suffer from NPD laugh at suggestions of therapy. I'm certain a high-test score could sway a few of them, but the majority simply can't imagine allowing someone else to scrutinize their life.

Narcissists have to stay in control if they want to keep the fantasy of their power and influence alive. Once that person is diagnosed, the control goes to the score—the adjudicator. To a person with NPD, that's a living nightmare.

It's a shame because those with this disorder stand to gain so much from proper treatment. Imagine if that confidence and intelligence could go toward something positive—it would be mind-boggling!

I want to break down the general traits of a narcissist. I imagine you bought this book because you already know you're living with one, but if you're uncertain, here's a quick rundown of clear giveaways.

EXPECTATIONS

More than anything, a narcissist expects you to treat them as if they're special. Don't ever assume they can manage driving through traffic. No—they must be alerted hours ahead of time, so they can make an intelligent detour and leave the gridlock to the plebians. It's your fault if they're late on that detour.

As you've probably noticed with this example, you'll find that narcissists have near-impossible standards. They'll expect everyone around them to work much harder and faster to ensure their comfort and give them a day free of friction. Anyone who lets them down will hear about it, usually at full volume.

One of my research volunteers told me about a boss she had who seethed anytime someone included the "I emailed you that already" message. He felt he shouldn't waste a moment digging through old emails, even if they were only from that morning.

"I got my butt handed to me last week because he asked for something I'd sent over and over. I resent it once, only to receive the same, 'Where's that email?' message from him again. I told him, 'You have it. I just sent it to you.' He marched over to my desk and publicly lectured me about my unprofessional behavior and unwillingness to be a team player.

"I just stared at him with my mouth open. All this because I mentioned he already had something in his inbox? I couldn't quit fast enough."

That boss' behavior reflects a narcissist's worldview perfectly. You don't tell me where something is—you bring it to me. Now. The public lecture and humiliation is another tactic we'll explore in depth later in this book.

EXAGGERATION

A narcissist looks in the mirror and sees someone special. There, in the glass, is the world's smartest, handsomest, and most influential person.

To the mind of an extreme narcissist, it's a true tragedy that they're yet to be famous and are still undiscovered. If only the world knew what it was missing!

In reality, most narcissists are smart, though not exceptional. Sure, they went to school and got a degree—the whole song and dance. But they see those accomplishments as hard proof that they're more special than you and everyone else around them.

Any narcissist confronted with the truth—that they're smart but not necessarily a *genius*—would crumble at the facts. Narcissists need their facades. They protect them from the real world and keep vulnerability at a distance.

MANIPULATION

One of the things that makes a person with NPD so dangerous is their willingness to use people. A high-scoring narcissist finds it very amusing when someone does as they command. They might talk someone out of applying for a promotion or into missing an opportunity to date their crush.

A narcissist does this because it gives them a boost of confidence. Unfortunately, it's a false confidence that will leave them feeling empty shortly after, so they have to do it again at the first opportunity.

This happens so consistently that most narcissists become professional manipulators. They can get most people to do just about anything, all while also making them believe it was their choice. It's also why someone with this personality disorder scares us—someone who can convince us to do any number of things could make us break the law or lie to a person we love. They can make us unlock the door when it should stay closed and barricaded.

Manipulation deserves to be taken seriously, and it's something we have to learn to recognize and stop in its tracks as soon as possible.

THIN-SKINNED

The trait that made me want to study NPD and those who suffer from it was their sensitivity.

At first glance, it seems out of place. After all, these are people who get others to do whatever they say, constantly tell themselves they're special, and demand compliments. With that hard work, it would seem impossible that their feelings could ever get hurt.

Oh, but they do. There is no one more sensitive or quick to injure than a true narcissist.

It makes sense once you see their confidence and self-assuredness as it is: a thin veneer draped over constant self-doubt. It's so thin that any level of criticism or attempt to stand up to them is instantly met with rage. They can lash out in a nanosecond, and their aim is precise.

The reason narcissists work so hard for special treatment—for pedestals to stand on and adoring fans—is their insecurity. They can't stand themselves without all of those props and an audience ready to jump to their feet in a standing ovation.

A narcissist alone is a person in deep self-hate and true sadness.

Don't believe me? Try calling the narcissist in your life insecure. Then, you can stand back and watch the fireworks.

WHAT MOTIVATES A NARCISSIST?

Why all this hard work to feel just a little bit special or smarter than the average person? Why do narcissists push day and night to get what they want?

A narcissist's deepest motive is never letting anyone know how insecure they feel. That's a terrible secret that they work day and night to keep hidden. So, most of what a narcissist would say or do is often geared toward hiding that side of themselves.

Narcissists also work hard to look good on every level. They might spend hours in a gym to keep a trim waistline or defined muscles. Or, they might spend far too much on clothes and accessories. Hair care is non-negotiable; they want to stand out everywhere they go.

My friend, Angie, remembers seeing her father in a department store, grabbing fancy shirts and piling them onto his arm.

"He had so many he could roll them up into a colorful log. He carried them up to pay and my mom stopped him, explaining that there was no way we could afford the massive amount of clothes he was hauling. He *lost* it! He had to have every single one of those shirts, no compromise.

"Luckily, my mom put her foot down. Us kids needed school clothes and supplies, meaning those came first. My dad stormed out and sat in the car while us kids got a few outfits each. He fumed all the way home.

"I was little, but even then, I thought, 'Wow, my dad just had a tantrum.'"

Angie's father's need to buy excessive amounts of fancy clothes is a perfect example of the narcissist's constant maintenance on his self-image. That work extends into how others perceive them. Narcissists want to be respected, even revered, whenever possible. If a narcissist is a decent guitar player, for example, they'll keep their guitar out where any visitors might see it and take every chance to play it or talk about their talent. If they're in a band, they'll want tons of solos so the audience can shriek with joy as they play.

Attention is a narcissist's bread and butter. They won't do anything if no one will see them. Why help someone if no one is looking? Why get a job with no opportunity for recognition? No, the narcissist wants to ensure that they have an audience, even a small one, before they do you a favor or put in any extra effort at the office.

Once a narcissist gets eyes and ears on their actions and words, they start to feel worthy of the praise. Without it, their guarded insecurities surface, and they'll do anything to beat it back down.

All of this affects how a narcissist relates to others. Their relationships exist to make them look good and no one else. Their thin veneer of false self-confidence can come crumbling down at any moment, and they *have* to be in complete control of their date or partner.

That means the narcissist has to assert themselves in small ways and keep anyone close to them in check. Imagine you're on a date with a narcissist and they mispronounce a word on the menu. Say they accidentally say, "monster cheese" when they meant to say "muenster." It happens, right? You politely correct them with a casual, "Actually that's 'muenster.' It's delicious. You should try it."

In your mind, you might give this all of two seconds of thought. To a narcissist, this is all part of your evil plot.

The narcissist sees the world as a place filled with landmines and enemies. Moments like the cheese incident are proof that everyone around them is dying to laugh in their face and idiocy. The whole world wants them to be wrong and wrong constantly.

Although a balanced person wouldn't give your comment much attention, a narcissist will be completely unable to let it go. They'll look for any opportunity to shoot you down through the rest of dinner. They'll silently beg you to mispronounce something, then tear your confidence to shreds. As far as they're concerned, it's all fair game. After all, you started it.

Narcissists rarely consider the long-term consequences of their actions, particularly when they have to do with others' emotions. If your date ends with you in tears, the narcissist won't give it too much thought. The important thing is that they're right and left feeling good about themselves. If you can't control your emotions, well, that's not their problem.

If a statement like this drives you away and makes you never want to spend another moment with your former date, they still won't feel bad about their actions. Rather, they'll see you as someone they managed to escape—that horrible person who tried to embarrass them in a restaurant.

Ask them for a conversation about the incident, and they'll do everything they can to avoid it. No narcissist wants to develop their introspection. That's a terrifying notion to most of them because one look inside will show them how much fear they carry inside. They're not a swaggering, good-looking superstar; they're a trembling child desperate to be loved. One glance might be all that true self needs to come out.

To keep from looking inside, narcissists will do anything they can to sidestep boredom. They want to be surrounded by people, constantly on adventures, and on the hunt for the next big thing. This can make a narcissist a lot of fun to hang out with on a Friday night, but a nightmare on Saturday morning when all you want to do is sleep, and your narcissist friend is bounding around your apartment, looking for something to do.

A narcissist can be a great friend as long as they see you as someone who will get them what they want. Most narcissists see their social group, romantic partners, or family members as special tools to unlock the life they want. And narcissists always want; they're never satisfied.

Controlling people is a 24-hour job, so they will use a set of tactics to keep everyone around them working toward the narcissist's goals.

THE NARCISSIST'S TACTICS

A narcissist works hard to make sure anyone close to them doesn't have their own interests or identity. If that happens, those people might forget to work on making them comfortable, giving them attention, and making them feel valued. Any sign that a partner or close friend has other things to do besides shower the narcissist with their attention and energy is dangerous and has to be shut down immediately.

The moment someone close to them needs to go to a special event, requires time alone, or wants to pursue a creative hobby like swing dancing or oil painting, the narcissist starts to get nervous.

They see that time and energy put into those activities or spent on your own as a threat to their delicate veneer of happiness. Thus, they'll start to make threats. These threats can be covert, disguised as something else like a request or concern, or overt, as in, you're doing this to avoid me.

I had this issue with my own girlfriends on many occasions. One partner—Jan—seemed particularly put off by my study group. She insisted that one of the girls there had a "major crush" on me, and my attending was proof that I wanted to mislead the poor girl into thinking I loved her.

"Nothing like that is happening," I explained in my calmest voice. "We have a test coming up and I need to study. That's all."

Nope, not good enough—once her original threat didn't hold, she resorted to another move straight out of the narcissist's playbook: name-calling.

"You are such a needy little prick," she hissed at me. I felt so shocked that I staggered back a bit. Needy? For wanting to study for a test? At the time, I felt genuinely confused and made the mistake of fighting back, which was exactly what she wanted.

That name-calling tactic has a goal: narcissists want the people around them to abandon their personal lives, separate identities, and sense of self-worth by arguing with them. If we're busy fighting with our partner or family member about their image of us, we're not out living our lives. The point goes to the narcissist.

Narcissists also keep us in check by making sure we never *quite* meet their standards. Every attempt we make is picked apart and held up as proof that we don't really love our partner or value our friend. No, nothing is good enough, and the narcissist will make sure you know that at every opportunity.

You'll see it when you give a narcissist a gift. Rather than a genuine, "thank you!" you'll be more likely to get a sniffed, "oh, great," or something similar. Later, you'll see the present abandoned on a table and have to hear about how you should know better than to give them something blue/antique/cheap etc. Don't you know them at all?

This constant beat down of your judgment and ability to make choices keeps your sense of self-worth low. It ensures you'll work harder to prove your love and adoration of the narcissist at every opportunity, while abandoning any other interests you had before.

Of course, all that work to prove you are on the narcissist's side will amount to nothing. Once a narcissist has someone hooked, they will keep them wriggling with blanket statements about their character.

After I skipped my study session and barely got a C on my exam, Jan made sure to let me know that I "didn't take responsibility for anything," and "could never concentrate on tests." I took that hard. School was my first joy, and it hurt terribly to hear someone whittle me down to a bad student who didn't understand that studies were important.

The comment made me evaluate my relationship with Jan. I'll take a lot from a partner, but get between me and my education, and we have a problem. The afternoon I received my test score, I mumbled some excuse about needing to get back to my place, and then avoided her calls for the next couple of days.

On day three, I got a knock on my door—it was my friend Trent from my cognitive psychology class. I was shocked to see him, since Trent and I never hung out at my place. I waved him in anyway.

"What brings you here?"

"Um," Trent blushed and looked down at the carpet. "Jan asked me to come check on you? To see if you're okay? I don't know. She made it sound like you were super depressed or something."

I assured Trent that I did not have any symptoms of depression. What I had was a girlfriend who kept me from studying and earned me a low C in a class where I desperately needed the A. Trent and I hung out at a nearby bar and talked it all over. It appeared she'd gotten a third person involved in an attempt to make me prove not just to her, but to everyone else too that I was in a healthy, happy relationship.

This move is called triangulation. Jan's claim that I was "depressed", and she was "worried" about me were meant to make me worry that perhaps I wasn't feeling quite right. Narcissists love making their partners or family members question their own sanity. It puts the narcissist right in the driver's seat and makes them look like a saint for being concerned in the first place.

Jan's attempt at getting me to run back to her backfired. Like me, Trent studied human behavior and encouraged me to end it with my girlfriend.

"It's concerning that she had no problem getting me involved," he told me over our third beer. "And your reluctance to call her and make up? That's all the proof I need that it's over between you two."

I agreed and decided to do the hard thing: go to Jan's place and break up with her. I knew she'd have a million tricks up her sleeve to keep the breakup from happening, but I also knew it had to happen.

I arrived at Jan's place the next day. She answered the door with no makeup on and her hair pulled back into a simple ponytail.

"Where have you been? I called you so many times."

I didn't answer. Instead, I laid out the breakup. Our relationship was not working, and I wanted out. Jan cried delicate, tiny tears and made little, sad sniffs.

"You're the best thing that ever happened to me," she said. "You're so handsome and smart. You're the most intelligent guy I know. And I love how you…"

She went on and on about all of my great qualities, a list I would have loved to hear during the actual relationship. At the moment, I saw her efforts to win me back as what they were: a love bomb.

Narcissists use love bombs as a way to make us feel lifted up and special in their eyes. How could you leave me? I adore you!

This happens when we first meet a narcissist who wants us in their lives, romantically or otherwise. It also happens when we take the reins and try to regain control once we see the relationship is toxic and hurting us more than helping.

Luckily for me, I was so fed up with Jan and our rollercoaster of a relationship that her love-bombing didn't work. I repeated myself, "I'm done. We're through," and walked away. She didn't call me after that, but she did make sure to parade her new boyfriend around the next day so I could see that she'd moved on.

Jan's attempt to love-bomb me during the breakup made me roll my eyes a bit. All the things she'd criticized only days before had apparently melted away, and suddenly I was the perfect man. What happened to all of my faults?

The love bomb both reaffirms and depletes the relationship. Once it detonates, it spins around the victim, leaving the poor recipient trapped in conflicting messages and dizzy with confusion. A love bomb tells you that you are loved, yet leaves you sore with injuries and makes your ears ring from all the noise. It's meant to get you back to the beginning of the relationship, so you'll bend over backwards to make the narcissist happy.

Other narcissist tactics include word salad and projection. They often blend together in an attempt to exhaust a family member or partner into throwing their hands into the air and forfeiting the fight. Instead of talking about the issue at hand, the narcissist will throw any and all topics into the fray, desperate to distract the other party into forgetting the real problem. Tossed into the mix will be phrases like "You're so mean!" or "Why are you so insecure?"

Remember that narcissists love to make others doubt their reality at every opportunity. Once your motives and actions are called into question, you'll either defend yourself or question your reality. That's a big win for a narcissist.

The tactic I want to delve into the most throughout this book is gaslighting.

Gaslighting is a common move meant to throw the spotlight on an innocent person and works to erode that individual's sanity. It's a horrible, insidious play, and if you don't know how to recognize it, you can easily fall prey to its effects.

Gaslighting happens all too often and can eat away at your self-esteem long after you've removed yourself from a dangerous situation. As a victim of razor-sharp gaslighting myself, I want to help you avoid or heal from this mental attack and become a stronger, more self-assured person.

But first, we need to investigate what gaslighting is and how it pulls us apart.

CHAPTER SUMMARY

You're on your way to a healthy understanding of narcissism and how to keep it at arm's length. Here's what we have covered so far:

- People with narcissistic traits fall on a spectrum.
- A person with narcissistic tendencies isn't necessarily dangerous.
- Narcissistic Personality Disorder (NPD) keeps a person from living a full life and functioning properly in society.

In the next chapter, we'll look closer at how a narcissist gaslights people and keeps them under their control.

2

WHAT IS GASLIGHTING?

The term "gaslighting" comes from a 1930's hit play adapted into a couple of movies, the most famous one being *Gaslight*. In it, a beautiful Ingrid Bergman falls victim to the handsome Charles Boyer, who plays a narcissist with a rather chilling precision that will make your skin crawl.

Charles' character Gregory meets and romances the beautiful opera singer Paula. He marries her after just two weeks of non-stop wooing, and then moves her into an old, abandoned house in London. However, Gregory is secretly a killer and has to ensure that Paula never finds out about his past.

To do this, he convinces her that she's going insane. A brooch disappears from her bag, and then a picture vanishes from the wall. Beyond that even, his favorite trick is to make the flames in the house's *gas lights* dim and brighten seemingly by magic.

Whenever Paula would say something, Gregory would insist he saw nothing with the lights, adding that things are disappearing thanks to her bizarre tendency to steal and hide precious objects. As a result, Paula starts to wonder if she is crazy—she can't remember taking anything and can't explain what she's seen.

I won't spoil the ending here, but I'm certain that you can see some classic narcissist moves in Gregory from that brief summary. I've seen the movie once out of curiosity, but I doubt I'll sit through it again. Although it is a stunning film and definitely worth a watch, I found it horribly triggering.

Gregory's stance, hard stare, and constant insistence that poor Paula was losing her mind all set my teeth on edge. It felt horribly familiar, particularly the gaslighting on Gregory's part. Let's get into it.

WHAT IS GASLIGHTING?

I want to clarify that gaslighting is abuse. It is an emotional and psychological beating that can leave a victim scarred and uncertain of their own reality for years to come. I don't want you to fall into or stay in the terrible cycle of gaslighting because it can do horrible things to your stress level, fear, anxiety, and sanity.

Someone who gaslights another person, such as a child, partner, or family member, wants to make that person question their sanity, memories, or perception of reality. Like Gregory playing with the lights or making objects disappear, it's a ploy to make a person feel powerless in the world and their relationship. A successful attempt at gaslighting ends with one person telling the other what's real, what their opinion should be, and what they remember. Let someone gaslight you long enough, and you'll atrophy into a kind of zombie bumping around in the world.

Plenty of people with NPD use gaslighting to keep their partners and those close to them wondering if they did in fact say or do something awful, but it's not their only move. Gaslighting is one of many ways a person with NPD will control others around them, though it is a good sign that a person is not someone you should get close to romantically.

The reason I feel so strongly about gaslighting and worked so hard in my career to help people see it is because it's a weapon. This thing causes damage, but it also violates the love and trust you've given to your partner or friend. It looks at your affection and sees a chance to twist it into a shiv that can cut you deeply and leave you bleeding for years, wondering where it all went wrong.

Gaslighting can be hard to recognize and even harder to name because it comes from someone we love. A stranger or new acquaintance doesn't know enough about us to truly get into our psyche. No, it's the ones we hold dear and stand beside who take advantage of our love.

One of my study subjects, Renee, had a boyfriend whom she'd dated since she was 16. She adored him, although she admitted he "had a temper."

"He got mad at me the other night about something," she told me. "But honestly, I completely overreacted and made a fool of myself in the restaurant." When I pressed for details, Renee seemed reluctant to tell me what her long-time boyfriend had done. Finally, after some gentle probing, I got her to admit that he'd insulted her weight, (despite her not being heavy), and made her feel ugly. The moment she got understandably upset at the insult, he informed her she was making a scene and insisted they leave. He stormed out as Renee quickly paid the bill for a meal they didn't even get a chance to eat.

"But we're fine now," she assured me. I asked a couple of questions about how they were suddenly fine. Had they discussed the argument and reached a compromise? The question made Renee look at me like I had switched from English to Latin.

"We're just, you know…" She shrugged. "Fine."

Renee's date insisting her getting emotional over something that most of us would take to heart is a common aspect of gaslighting. Any reaction, despite how nuanced or reasonable, is instantly labeled "crazy" or somehow over the line by a narcissist. The other's take on the situation, like being publicly insulted, is instantly negated.

I don't think Renee's boyfriend actually wanted her to lose any weight or rethink her diet. I think he saw her confidence growing and decided to shoot her down. I'm sorry to say he succeeded.

WHO BECOMES A GASLIGHTER?

Gaslighting tends to appear in people who have a personality disorder, and NPD in particular. However, it also appears in psychopaths, who are individuals that can't empathize with others.

We have to keep in mind that the person doing the gaslighting is hiding something. They aren't all necessarily secret criminals like

Gregory in the movie, but they each have a terrible secret. They're insecure, and some sick part of themselves believes that making someone who trusts and loves them feel terrible will build them up.

A practiced gaslighter has a public and a private face. I met Renee's boyfriend one day on my way to the library and chatted with him for a moment. He spoke with the ease and charm I found common among people with NPD. His hair had a nice wave in it, and he had pretty blue eyes. He treated me like someone he admired after a quick intro-duction, and I'm sure he would have kept up the facade if I'd hung out longer than I did.

However, I wasn't fooled. I knew for a fact that he treated Renee like dirt, despite her love for him. Like so many other manipulators, this guy felt the need to make sure that if Renee were ever to talk about the terrible things he did, she'd find herself faced with doubt.

To the mind of the narcissist, if they're nice to everyone else and only mean to their partner, the partner will have no one to turn to for help or support. Unfortunately, this tactic works quite often, though I find that now people tend to be more suspicious of overly charming people. We have enough evidence that the most beautiful and winning of those around us can also be the most dangerous, so atti-tudes are gradually shifting.

The more practiced gaslighters—the real pros—are the hardest to detect. They're extremely careful when in the company of anyone not close to them and make sure to be polite yet not lay it on too thick. They've struck a delicate balance that makes it much harder for anyone outside of their closest relationships to see their true selves.

Only their partners and families get to see the darkness they carry and often have no one to turn to for help.

WHY DO PEOPLE GASLIGHT OTHERS?

In order to understand this behavior, you have to step back and look at how gaslighting benefits that person who insists on treating others around them so terribly.

On a basic level, it helps them gain control. The person they've torn down will either question themselves, doubt something they know to be true, or leave. All scenarios are a win for the manipulator; the first two give them a willing participant whom they can continue to control, and the last gives them someone who sees their true personality out of their circle, allowing them to avoid accountability.

Over time, constant gaslighting creates codependency. Imagine every time someone asked you to do a math problem, and each time you worked it out, you got it wrong. After a while, you'd stop trying to solve math problems. Instead, you'd turn to someone else for help or guidance, certain you can't handle it on your own.

That's exactly what a gaslighter wants. They need you to see them as a guide through life, a professional to hold your hand as you stumble along. This experience makes the narcissist drunk with power. They will see themselves as a genius, able to string along partners so they will do whatever they say, whenever they give the command.

The high that comes with such an immense amount of control can be as addictive as alcohol or an opiate. Power makes people hungry for more power, even if they only wield it over one individual.

There's a radio story on the show *This American Life* called "Chip in My Brain," which fascinated me to no end. I listened to it over and over because it picked apart an instance of something called a one-on-one cult, which is an unusual occurrence. It happens when someone learns a few psychological tricks, then pulls them on an individual, convincing them that the leader is aware of a danger and happens to be the only person with the information to keep that member safe.

I won't go into the details of the story; I only mention it because the story's producer, David Kestenbaum, got the cult leader, a man in his thirties named A.J., to sit down for an interview. A.J. had recently been found guilty of intentional infliction of emotional distress in court and wasn't too happy about it. In the interview with the radio producer, A.J. gaslights like crazy.

Kestenbaum asked a direct question about A.J.'s religious beliefs, and A.J. would deflect in response. "Explain. I don't understand." Then, he redirected again. "Well, let me ask you about radios…" Over and over, A.J. refused to state what he believes or why he believes in it.

At every opportunity, A.J. would laugh out loud at a question, trying to make Kestenbaum feel stupid for even considering asking. But the producer held firm. He asked the question simply and directly. "What do you believe?" Unfortunately, he never really received an answer, but I expected A.J., a true manipulator, to refuse to state his beliefs plainly.

A.J. found young men as his easiest targets and did horrific, psychological damage to one in particular. The poor kid developed such a deep fear of demons and impending death that he missed out on a great trip to England. In college, he slept under his bed in the dorm; it made him feel safe to curl up in the tiny space.

It took years of therapy and endless love and patience from his family to bring him back to his normal self, but he still missed years of school and childhood happiness thanks to one ongoing gaslight session.

WOULD A NARCISSIST TARGET YOU?

If you're going to be on the lookout for others anxious to take advantage of your kind nature, you have to ask yourself about the qualities you have that might make you a prime target.

Consider how you talk about yourself. Do you have faith in yourself as a person, or do you put yourself down and insult yourself or your work? Do you have a hard time saying no to others, particularly if you see them as smarter, better looking, or better than you in general?

These habits can open our front door to dangerous people. When others hear us disrespecting ourselves, they see either a sad case or an opportunity to get what they want.

Other bad habits that can allow a gaslighter into your life include taking on too much or refusing to say no to someone who needs help, even if you have no time. The second action is a symptom of people-pleasing. It's a nice habit on the surface, but it's a rose-tinted view of a lack of self-respect. If you value yourself as a person, you value your time and self-care. When others see that you put yourself last, they'll follow your example.

Please don't misunderstand me—I am not blaming victims in any way. Rather, I want to alert you that some of your bad habits could attract toxic people. I want you to take care of yourself and keep yourself safe however you can.

We'll get deeper into how you can love yourself if you're in a bad situation or get out of one in a later chapter. For now, just know that you're a wonderful person and you deserve better.

Gaslighting Techniques

Withholding

Withholding references a narcissist's tendency to refuse to acknowledge another's emotions. It can also present itself as a refusal to listen.

You'll hear it in phrases like, "What do you mean?" or "You're not making any sense." These attempts to redirect the conversation get the narcissist's partner to focus on being clear rather than the actual problem.

Countering

Whenever you remember something clearly, but someone insists that thing never happened, you're experiencing a counter.

Remember the lights dimming and brightening in *Gaslight*. This move is intended to make the victim doubt her sanity and it often works. Modern versions of that move tend to focus on whether someone said or did something. A narcissist will insist you "never remember our conversations," or "it's only in your head."

I can remember constantly wishing for a stenographer or Dictaphone to have proof that what I remembered matched up with reality. If you've felt that way with anyone, you're dealing with someone who can counter masterfully.

Forgetting/Denial

A small step down from countering, the denial move helps a narcissist feel absolved of any responsibility.

This happens when a narcissist is reminded of a promise or held to their word. Suddenly, all memory of the narcissist's former commitment vanishes.

The phrase, "I never said that," will be on repeat for most narcissists.

My own mom perfected denial. One minute I was promised a day in the park, but when I asked about it, I'd be informed that I'd imagined the conversation. Worse, my mom could pretend not to hear me and refuse to address the question. As a little boy, it broke my heart.

When I was in middle school and desperately wanted to make friends, my mom would promise me an afternoon to myself. The moment I put on my shoes to meet up with other boys for a round of video games, she'd look at me and ask, "Where are you going?" I'd explain, only to be told that she'd never agreed to let me leave.

It didn't take long for me to learn to stop asking. Instead of telling my mom where I wanted to go and when, I'd avoid going home at all.

Instead, I'd go to a friend's place after school and hang out as long as they'd let me. By the time I got home, I had to face my furious mother, but at least I made friends.

Trivializing

I put this one on a higher level than many, but that's because I find it extremely dangerous. Trivializing happens any time someone minimizes how you feel.

A narcissist will tell you something like, "Oh, you got those ideas from your mom. You know she's nuts," or something along those lines.

Unlike countering, trivializing makes the recipient doubt if the narcissist is manipulating them, if maybe someone else is to blame. This kind of behavior keeps a lot of good people in terrible relationships, since they will start to see everyone who wants to help them as the true danger.

Don't underestimate this one; it can turn your life inside out.

Lying

In my book, there are two groups who can lie better than anyone: addicts and narcissists.

In both cases, the liar convinces everyone around them so well that anyone who hears them will start to question themselves and their versions of the truth.

This happens because the person telling the lie is terrified of the truth. Should they say even one honest word, they'll be ruined. Fear makes them dig their heels in and stand on the flimsy lie for years, no matter what gets proven. If they insist it's true, they'll pray and avoid rehab or facing their true, cowardly self.

Discrediting You to Others

I believe to discredit the same person you claim to love is the lowest move out there. A narcissist sees this incredibly underhanded play and thinks, "I can do that."

This is a long con. Your narcissist partner or relative will feign concern for you while dropping hints that you are "unstable" or calling you "crazy" to anyone in your personal network. This works as a defense in case you go to anyone for help.

In the narcissist's mind, your attempts at finding any support from friends, family, or other groups will be tutted away. "Oh, he told me she was crazy," they'll say while shaking their heads at you.

Real life often doesn't work this way. Some people sway easily, sure, but most of those I know don't pay too much attention when a person who should be able to function in society is written off as "crazy." Yet, it often doesn't matter. If the victim of emotional abuse already believes they have no one to turn to, they'll stay with their abuser and never seek help.

Weaponizing Compassion

It's hard, immediately after someone's hurt you, when they insist, "I would never do that on purpose!" or "That's just how I am sometimes. I was raised like this."

These are attempts to make a victim's compassion bubble up and turn anger into understanding, even when the narcissist does real harm. Most narcissists target exceptionally kind and generous people because they see an opportunity to take that kindness and sharpen it to a point. You're kind? What happens when I stab at you with your own emotion, then tell you it's not my fault? Are you still a nice person?

To have our own emotions used against us can feel terrifying. Instead of standing up for ourselves we start to see ourselves as mean, uncaring, even evil. Again, this takes the pressure off the narcissist. They can feel free to strut away from any problem, no matter how badly destroyed he's left the one he loves.

Twisting and Reframing

To take a situation and twist it around, then reframe it so someone else gets the blame, is the narcissist's bread and butter. "I didn't do it!" they'll say. "I was there, standing innocently by while all those terrible things happened. How can you accuse me?"

An example of this is physical abuse. If your partner shoves you down a couple of steps, then you confront them, their defense will be to turn everything on to you.

"No, no! I didn't push you. I saw you were about to trip, and I caught you. Your shoe caught on something, that's all."

And there goes the last of your confidence in yourself.

COMMON GASLIGHTING PHRASES

There are many tools in a gaslighter's toolbox. Here, I've compiled a set of phrases that tend to get thrown around often by these people.

- You're so sensitive!
- You know that's just because you are so insecure.
- Stop acting crazy. / You sound crazy, you know that, don't you?
- You are just paranoid.
- You just love trying to throw me off track.
- I was just joking!
- You are making that up.
- It's no big deal.
- You're imagining things.
- You're overreacting.
- You are always so dramatic.
- Don't get so worked up.
- That never happened.
- You know you don't remember things clearly.
- There's no pattern. / You are seeing a pattern that isn't there.
- You're hysterical.
- There you go again, being so ungrateful.
- Nobody believes you, so why should I?
- If you were paying attention… / If you were listening… / If you knew how to listen…
- We talked about this. Don't you remember?
- You're being irrational.

- You can't take a joke.
- Why would you say that? What does that say about you?
- Why are you upset? I was only kidding.
- I'm not arguing; I'm discussing.
- I criticize you because I like you.
- You're reading too much into this.
- You're the only person I have these problems with.
- Stop taking everything I say so seriously.
- You always jump to the wrong conclusions.

HOW TO KNOW IF YOU ARE A VICTIM OF GASLIGHTING

Imagine the narcissist in your life finds out you bought this book. Maybe they discover you reading it. What would they say?

If you immediately imagine them laughing at your silly purchase, ridiculing this text, and questioning your judgment for being suckered, you have a narcissist on your hands.

Other signs are bountiful in number, but I believe in my heart that when someone is in a bad relationship of any kind, the truth lives in their hearts. A realistic person would ask concerned questions if they saw a book you wanted to read. They might say, "You think someone is gaslighting you? Who? Can I help? Have I said something?" Those loving, helpful responses show that that person truly cares for you and knows that a relationship involves self-reflection.

On the other hand, narcissists ensure that those mature conversations never leave your imagination. I want you to read through the following checklist and see how many of these statements line up with how you feel with your partner, family member, or friend. If one person in your life makes you think or stress over any of the following, it's time to take action.

Start here:

When I'm with _____, I...

- ...ask myself whether I'm just being too sensitive.
- ...feel confused, sometimes even crazy in this relationship.
- ...am always apologizing.
- ...can't understand why I'm not happier with them.
- ...frequently make excuses for their behavior.
- ...know something's wrong, but I just can't figure out what.
- ...lie or omit facts to avoid being insulted or hearing my version twisted.
- ...have trouble making decisions.
- ...feel withdrawn; I don't want to call or see anyone.
- ...feel an impending sense of doom.
- ...wonder if I'm good enough.
- ...doubt my perceptions of a time/place/situation and personal judgments.

Any more than three agreements to the above statements should be considered as a clear red flag that you're dealing with a narcissist and it's time to start putting yourself first. You can't let someone steal your sense of self. That part of you holds your key to a happy life.

The person you thought of when taking that quiz—the one who would happily tear this book to shreds—is likely a narcissist. That narcissist is also the person you need to rid from your life.

CHAPTER SUMMARY

In this chapter, we picked apart some big topics.

- Narcissists of all kinds tend to rely on the same set of tactics.
- Gaslighting has a unique history and specific use to make the victim doubt their own mind.
- We can recognize different signs identifying when someone is gaslighting us.

In the next chapter, we'll take a closer look at how gaslighting happens from beginning to end.

3

THE STAGES OF GASLIGHTING

You might ask yourself how anyone can end up with a partner who gaslights them regularly. You may feel confident that you could never be a victim of this behavior. You might think, "thank goodness that's not me," when you read about an abusive relationship. What kind of person could possibly allow themselves to end up in this scenario, anyway?

Unfortunately, harmful relationships often feel healthy when they're clearly not, especially at the beginning.

I like to give this example; imagine you and someone close to you have to share a bed. It's gorgeous—the style you love, all your favorite colors for sheets and pillows, and the mattress feels perfect on your back. At the end of the day, you can't wait to snuggle into it and drift off to sleep.

At first, you and your partner share the mattress equally. Then, one morning, you realize your section is a tiny bit smaller than it was last night. But oh well, these things happen. However, each day, you wake up to find your section just a touch smaller than it was the night before.

Your partner, meanwhile, gets more and more of the mattress. After a few weeks, they're spread out like a starfish while you hang onto the edge, desperate to get back into that beautiful sleeping arrangement you had at the start.

The worst part of it happens when you try to bring up your shrinking section. Any time you defend your side, you have to hear about how it isn't a big deal, then how it's in your mind, and suddenly, you get called insane for mentioning a bed at all. Never mind that it's directly under you.

That's the easy breakdown of how gaslighting builds one move at a time. Let's get into the technical part of how narcissists find a partner, then pull them into a dangerous situation one step at a time.

STAGES OF THE RELATIONSHIP

The first meeting of a narcissist and their new partner almost always looks like something out of a movie. The moment explodes with love. Many partners to narcissists remember the early days as perfect. Somehow, this new person in their lives knew exactly what to say and when to say it and swore they had feelings for them beyond anything they'd ever felt. Maybe they blushed during their first early confession of love.

"I know this is crazy," they'll admit, "but I can't deny it. I'm head over heels for you."

This is love-bombing, or the **Idealization Stage.** This stage helps narcissists draw in someone who is unsure of themselves. A confident partner won't need this much attention from someone new and might find it stifling. However, someone who's recently been hurt, has low self-esteem, or feels desperate for a partner will swoon at this kind of attention.

Many people I've spoken to describe this stage as "a dream." That tells me a lot. One piece of advice I can give is when something feels too good to be true, that's because it probably is.

A man I'll call Mark remembers meeting his former partner Bee and wondering how he could have gotten so lucky.

"It was like she could read my mind. I was in the mood for a beer when we met up at a coffee shop, and she looked at me and said, 'You want to head to the bar?' Then she matched me drink for drink, something I've always liked in women. It's silly, but I think of someone unafraid to drink as a person who grabs life by the horns.

"We went out for burgers, and it was great. We talked for hours. She seemed to intuit just what I wanted to hear. I remember at one point in the evening, she sat back, took me in, and said, 'You're the kind of guy I could commit to. I mean *really* commit. And I have options, Mark. I could walk out of here and find five men who'd love to take me home. But I won't. I want to stay right here for as long as you'll have me.'

"Words can't express what that little speech did to me mentally. I grabbed her hand, pulled her out into the street, and kissed her. My whole body vibrated. My heart couldn't stop leaping up in my chest. She felt magical."

That dreamlike feeling is our subconscious alerting us to an unrealistic standard. No one feels true love on the first date. We might feel attracted or drawn to someone, but an all-out profession of love or request for a commitment in the first meeting is dangerous.

Unfortunately for people like Mark, those early seductions are carefully calculated to draw in new partners and get them hooked. And they often work. A lot of narcissists have a set of phrases or practiced speeches like Bee's that they know will get the person interested and keep them wanting more.

The moment we look at these dream encounters realistically; we start to see the cracks. Why would someone want a relationship with a person they don't know? It's because they've sensed that this is a person with whom they can build codependency. They need this person to reassure themselves that they're the soon-to-be-discovered star they want to be, while the new partner can acquiesce their own confidence to build up the narcissist's self-worth.

Of course, this doesn't start right away. After a narcissist secures a promise of love or commitment, they can start to test their boundaries.

It's hard for a narcissist's partner to say what exactly it is they did the first time. All they know is that the narcissist shifted from a deep love to a nagging discomfort. A person who started out as a dream in the beginning may evolve into a partner with odd demands, strange claims, and an underlying need for constant attention.

They won't state anything outright. It could be a basic request for food. "I would love some scrambled eggs this morning," for example. Of course! Love to, darling. Their new partner quickly agrees and makes their version of scrambled eggs.

Several things might happen when the partner brings two plates to the table. The narcissist might take one bite and pull a face. They might blink in surprise and say, "That's how you do it?" or another comment meant to undermine the effort. Suddenly, their partner finds themselves apologizing for doing nothing wrong; they simply fulfilled a request. Instead of a thank you, they get a test.

Will they stand up for themselves or work to make the narcissist happy?

If the narcissist has chosen the correct partner—and they usually do—then they'll get the latter response. Instead of receiving a plate of eggs on their head for being a jerk, they'll get profuse promises that the next round will be better. The partner will try harder; they'll find a new recipe.

The partner will then probably rationalize the experience. Hey, they like their eggs a certain way. Some people are picky. Personal tastes are hard to punish. In the meantime, they're also trying not to tell themselves that they deserved a thank you and their eggs are delicious. They won't admit that their partner actually needs to apologize for their comments and walk out the door.

Instead, they work harder to make their partner happy. They were happy before, right? Wrong. The narcissist only presented a happy face to draw their partner in. Now, they can start the **Devaluation Phase.** After all, their first round of gaslighting their partner worked perfectly.

They've already introduced the false narrative of convincing their partner that their eggs are the problem, not the narcissist's lack of gratitude. That's a small taste of all the comments to come.

As the two of them spend more time together, the narcissist builds on that first disappointment. They'll sometimes look at their partner and ask, "Are you okay? You seem... I don't know... off." Their partner will take this to heart. Maybe they need to add an extra yoga class or therapy session to their regular regime. They wouldn't say those things if they weren't concerned, right?

The false narrative is an essential element to gaslighting. The narcissist wants their partner to feel like they fall short, no matter how hard they try. If they have a great job, the narcissist devalues the job and their role. They might pose questions like "How can you work at such a terrible place?" or "You know they underpay you, right?" no matter how much the partner likes their job.

One way a narcissist can steer a person's life into codependency is through money. If their partner leaves their job or allows them to decide how to spend their paycheck, they'll go broke and need the narcissist even more. From what I've seen in my own relationships, financial abuse is a small step away from emotional abuse. I don't mean that every narcissist uses it, only that it's an easy option.

This all feeds into the narcissist's ability to lie and exaggerate. Remember that narcissists will stand by a lie no matter what happens. To help build up a false narrative, they'll also exaggerate.

"You can't organize a closet to save your life!" they'll boom. Their partner might scramble to fix the problem, unaware that the narcissist barely even noticed their closet, and soon feel too exhausted to ask them what the fuss was about. Narcissists use this hyper focus on small matters to keep their partners emotionally worn down, too physically tired to fight back, and mentally distracted.

This second part of the relationship sees the narcissist become meaner and colder with each passing day. Nothing their victim does seems right, and they will run from one effort to another. No matter what they do, they never get home at the right time, none of their clothing looks good, and they always make the wrong jokes at parties.

All the narcissist's declarations of love are gone and replaced with criticisms and claims that their partner can't do anything, even listening to the narcissist the right way. The victim's life is now chaos. Every time they're heading home from work, they feel a gnaw in their stomach and their thoughts reel.

Will dinner be good enough? I asked them what they wanted, but what if I misheard them? Will they be happy about my progress at work or accuse me of devaluing their job again? Am I too hard on them? I must be. I don't know why I'm being so sensitive.

By the time they walk in the door, the victim doesn't know what to expect from their partner. They can almost visually see the eggshells littering the floor and the tiny spaces between them. It's up to the victim to navigate through this impossible set of obstacles without a single misstep.

The tragedy is that the victim's concentrated efforts only make the narcissist work harder to assure them that they're not good enough, mentally unstable, and no longer attractive. The gaslighting feeds off of itself and creates a whirl of chaos that swings both partners around. The victim only feels better when they get the odd kind word. The narcissist loves their constant efforts to be better but despises them for falling for their tricks.

One day, the partner finally snaps. They've caught the narcissist sexting another person while they washed all the dishes.

They hold up the phone and point to the message. What the *hell* is this?

To the victim's shock, their partner merely blinks in confusion.

"What are you talking about?" They show it to the narcissist again. Are they seriously denying what's right in front of them?

"I don't know anything about that. I'm not even sure why you're mad."

Their denial floors their partner. There, in that message, are some of the same sweet words that they got to hear once, a long time ago. Their partner could at least admit that they're flirting with someone else. Instead, they insist it never happened. They look at the evidence in their partner's hands and realize that they're in a truly bad situation.

After that fight, the narcissist's partner gets a moment of kindness. To their shock, the narcissist comes to them looking upset and apologizes.

"You're so wonderful. I hate to think I've hurt your feelings." They kiss their partner like they used to, and the partner gets a rush of that former love. The text message is forgotten, and the two go back to their evening, telling each other everything is fine.

To any outsiders, these two appear as what they are—codependent participants. Neither one is happy, yet no one wants to end the relationship. They both seem to want the rollercoaster of emotions and to get the rush of the high, despite the constant lows.

Finally, the narcissist can no longer look at the ruins of their former love. This feeling of utter disgust is called the **Discarding Phase.**

Now, the victim cannot do a single thing right. They no longer feel comfortable in their own home, which has become the lair of the person who drew them in, only to devour them like a vampire sucking out emotion.

The victim can see their partner's disinterest on their face, yet something makes them hold on to the hope that things can get better. They loved them once. What did they do to inspire so much passion and romance before? Can they recreate that same dynamic again?

The victim spends their days feeling confused, emotionally ragged, and desperate to fix whatever it is they think they broke. Our poor partner struggles to make their narcissist happy, but their last-ditch efforts to bring back the magic actually feeds the narcissist's ego, inspiring them to be worse on all fronts, continuing to wear the victim down.

There's little our victim can do, (or so they believe). Their power, respect, and safety are all in the narcissist's hands. Unless they grant their partner those things back, the partner will believe they can't have them. Now they're with someone who somehow got them to give up all their power, with no idea how to get it back.

But the victim does want it. They feel the door calling to them every day. Somehow, someday, they have to get out.

That's the moment I want you to feel. If you see yourself as powerless, in constant danger, and cringing to think of giving yourself a compliment, I want you to know there's still hope for you.

Relationships, like the ones I described, are all too easy to fall into and can seem impossible to leave, but you need to remember that nothing is impossible.

CHAPTER SUMMARY

This chapter walked us through the maze that makes up a codependent relationship. Here's what we saw:

- An unhealthy relationship can start with a love-bomb, which is an overly earnest expression of love and passion that may not really be as earnest as it seems.
- Gaslighting comes later and starts with small, easily dismissed comments.

- It isn't until deep into the narcissist's trap that their partner will realize they're actually in a toxic relationship.

In the next chapter, you will learn about different kinds of relationships in which gaslighting occurs, and what to watch out for as you open up to new people.

4

GASLIGHTING IN OTHER RELATIONSHIPS

I think most people expect or experience true narcissism from a romantic partner, but this unhealthy relationship can develop between any two people. Once two people establish a power dynamic, it's possible for one of them to exploit their relationship.

Perhaps you watched a friend couple up with someone so bad that they made you roll your eyes and wonder how much longer you'd have to put up with the jerk. You may have fallen into a bad relationship yourself and seen the sighs of relief once you left. People outside of an unhealthy relationship will find it easy to point fingers at someone else's pain, yet we all fall victim to the same tactics, particularly when they can sneak up from behind us. Do you know when to be on the defensive with a boss or one of your parents? What about a friend who seems to always get their way, even when all they want is to make a scene? Can our siblings exploit our love too?

We need to know what a narcissistic gaslighting element looks like in all relationships so we can call them what they are: toxic. Once we see the truth behind a difficult relationship, we can find ways to separate ourselves from the person causing damage in our lives.

I want to explore some of these unique relationships in our lives that can change how we live and love. It's my goal to get everyone speaking openly about these situations, so we won't laugh at or shrug off someone who's in pain. Instead, we can speak to them as an informed friend or family member and help them see the truth.

A PARENT OR CAREGIVER

Most people I know had parents who hoped to see their children leave home eventually. These kids grew up to further their studies, start businesses, fall in love, and build their own lives.

We assume that most parents want their kids to grow into healthy, functioning adults. We hope the same for anyone in a foster home or living with relatives who took the place of Mom and Dad. Parenting isn't easy; we all know it can become abusive or dangerous, but it's harder to see the gaslighting that a parent gives a child.

When gaslighting comes from a mother, father, or caregiver, it focuses on making the victim feel inadequate, but in more basic ways than a romantic partner might. Children's lives have less nuance than adults, so the abuse follows suit.

My own mother liked to nitpick my tidiness, yelling "You call this a clean room?" It didn't matter how many hours I spent organizing, scrubbing, or making my bed—none of it ever met her standards. My A's in school also missed the mark, as school was, "dumbed down to make idiots feel smart."

Unrealistic chores and academic expectations are easy ways for a parent to shoot down their children. As a kid, I had no defense. Surely my mom knew what she was talking about—she'd already graduated from college after all. Her room stayed neat as a pin. Who was I to question her?

It's that dynamic gaslighting that a narcissistic parent depends on to keep the abuse alive. These parents make themselves the hero in their child's story—as in, I'm here to tell you the truth and show you what the world is really like.

Children don't question adults. Mom and dad are physically bigger, older, and supposedly smarter. The fact that a child has no bruises or marks to prove the abuse makes it much more difficult for others to spot the damage, and a child is unlikely to report these cutting remarks. They likely don't even realize they're being abused. To a kid, the treatment becomes normal quickly, and they assume everyone else's mom and dad act the same way.

This acceptance builds over the years with several tactics. Narcissist parents make sure their child has no oasis to turn to by invading their social life. My own mother often read my AIM notes from friends out loud in ridiculous voices, hoping to make my friends' words sound idiotic. It worked, unfortunately. I stopped logging on and kept to myself, giving her the chance to point out that she had an unpopular son.

One day in the third grade, I made the mistake of inviting a friend over. I say mistake because my mother put on a show like I'd never seen before. She came out with a plate of cookies, joined us in our video game, and pelted my friend with questions about his own mom. Before I knew it, my friend was running for the door, uncomfortable with my "weird mom" who seemed to think he had come to visit her.

"We'll go to your house next time," I assured him. But I didn't see much of him after that day. Of course, my mother let me know how it was actually me who didn't know how to host a visitor.

"You could learn a lot from me," she stated, arms crossed as she looked down at me. Exhausted, I agreed.

I can remember myself wondering if my mom might apologize once she realized my friend didn't want to see me anymore. But a narcissist never says they're sorry, and certainly not to a child. It was my hope that she might say it in private where no one else could hear, and I would promise never to repeat her heartfelt apology. Even then, I understood that for mom, it felt impossible to admit a mistake.

As an adult, I met lots of people who grew up in a home similar to mine. One or both of their parents denied them friendships, made them feel idiotic, or intruded in their personal space.

Some of their stories exemplify the gaslighting dynamic perfectly. I featured them here with names changed to protect their identities.

Robert (currently an owner of an electric car repair service)

Robert grew up in a wealthy family in Stonybrook. He could remember people in grocery stores or at church stopping his parents to comment on what beautiful kids he and his siblings were. People wanted to know where they shopped, who cut the kids' hair, and if they were so well-behaved because of a special nanny.

Families in their neighborhood worked tirelessly to keep up appearances. The pressure to be the right kind of family came to a head with their kids.

"My mom used to buy me designer polo shirts when I was a kid," Robert told me. "Designer clothes! For a little boy! It was insane. The name on the label gave her an excuse to never let me play outside. I couldn't run through the mud or skateboard with the other boys. They all came home muddy with skinned knees and messy hair. But my mom made sure to have receipts of how much my outfit cost so she could wave it in my face.

"'You get this dirty and you're paying for it!' she'd scream. In hindsight, I can see this was her way of keeping me inside with her all weekend. She must have felt terrified of me making friends—she literally *paid* to keep me alone.

"But nothing felt worse than when she compared me to my older brother, Sam. Everything Sam did made her happy. Sam ate the right amount of vegetables, cleaned his room before the maid came over (hired to make her job easier), and always had a smile on his face. Sam may as well have been canonized by the church. To Mom, he was a living saint.

"'Why can't you be more like Sam?' she'd sigh, looking at me with disgust. Then, one day, I was suddenly her little golden child, and Sam was out. And this is the worst part—I bought it. When Mom threw her arms around me and said, 'You're perfect, you know that?' my head spun around at full speed.

"For a few days, Sam was the one left behind when we went out for ice cream. Mom didn't want to check his homework and hated the way he dressed. I wish I could say I eventually came around, but I was a kid. I ate it up like a scoop of Rocky Road in a waffle cone.

"You won't be surprised to hear that it didn't last. It was never meant to—Mom just liked to play us off each other so we wouldn't get close. It worked, and Sam and I have a hard time hanging out, even now. As kids, we fought constantly. Mom would come break us up, and then instantly side with one or the other, leaving the other one in the cold.

"All of her hard work decimating my self-esteem made it difficult for me to try anything new. Even a future astronaut's group in school seemed too out of reach. But I loved science and math—it was a place where all the chaos disappeared, and I could be myself. At least I had the foresight not to show my enthusiasm for the logical world to my mom.

"I grew up convinced that everyone would compare me to someone else and find me disappointing. When I left home at 18, I remember feeling relieved once my mother cut me off so I couldn't access her money. Fine, I thought, give it to your angel, Sam.

"At my first garage, I expected everyone to laugh at me and wonder how I ever managed to do anything. But that didn't happen. I remember feeling shocked. Didn't they know what a loser they'd hired? I honestly felt the job they'd given me was some kind of charity, if you can imagine that. Getting respect from my colleagues opened my eyes like nothing else had in the past. I'm eternally grateful to them."

Betty

"My dad forbade me to express my emotions.

"He didn't exactly say, 'No emotions allowed.' Rather, if I tried to tell him I felt sad or confused, he'd wave his hands in front of his face, squeeze his eyes shut, and yell, 'I don't want to hear it!' Yet, his own anger, happiness, and even his tears meant we all had to give him our full attention. He liked to give these huge, meandering speeches, and if one of us dared to yawn or look out the window, he'd scream at us.

"The message came across loud and clear to me. He could have all the feelings, no one else. In that same vein, if he did anything, it was because one of us kids 'made' him do it. The first time I saw him hit my mom, he informed me that he'd only done it 'because you kids are so impossible.'

"That confused me endlessly. I remember lying in my bed, trying to work it out. I was young at the time—only about nine years old—and I didn't think to question Dad. Instead, I tried to remember what my siblings and I did to make him so angry at Mom.

"Of course, I never found an answer. What Dad wanted was for me to stay confused. He loved it when I had no idea what he meant or what was happening. He'd give me this poor-you expression and explain everything to me like I was the world's dumbest little girl. In fact, when I got good grades in school, he always insisted that I cheated, even though I never did.

"'Be sure to thank whoever it is that lets you copy off of him,' he would say. I didn't bother responding after the first fifteen times. I only said, 'I will,' and went off by myself.

"By then, Dad had lost all interest in me. I'd learned to ignore him, and he despised my ability to switch off his voice. He loved it whenever I got upset or desperate. But indifferent? He couldn't stand it. He'd take my brothers out for pizza and 'forget' to invite me, certain I'd lose it when they got home. Instead, I used the time alone in the kitchen to make something for myself. The sight of me eating a meal I'd cooked on my own made him seethe with anger.

"The abuse didn't stop with my mom. Dad also hit us kids, though he tended to target my brothers over me. I think he saw my lack of love for him early, so hitting me didn't feel worth his time. My brothers, however, adored him. Everything he did was endlessly cool. He played the guitar and rode a motorcycle. He left my mom for a younger woman with bigger boobs who agreed with everything he said. The few days he treated them kindly made up for all the bruises and insults he liked to keep fresh and painful.

"I tried to get some counseling in high school, but Dad shut that down right away. One of my brothers told him I'd been in the counselor's office for a session, and he went straight to my mom to punish her for my actions. He forced his way into Mom's house and smacked her across the face, then pointed at me.

"'Stop making me hit your mom!'

"I never went to a counselor after that. Even now, I'm terrified of therapists or anyone who works in psychology. Dad's gone, but that memory still haunts me.

"Long after Dad died, I found out his own father used to act the same way. I'd never met my grandfather; Dad always hated him and told us we should too. That was a big deal to me. I thought, *Whatever I do, I can't act like Dad.*

"That made me hyper aware of how I treated my boyfriends and my husband, and even my kids. Instead of therapy, I read tons of books about how to communicate, be open and honest, and keep accountability. Anything to keep from falling into Dad's traps.

"It's still a struggle. It's easy to point at others and insist your pain is their fault. It's much harder to look in the mirror and ask, 'What can I do to be a better person? What needs to change?' But trust me, it's worth it once you do it."

Dana

"My mom loved rules. She loved them so much that she made up new rules all the time, and that practice caused many to contradict the ones already in place. For instance, she insisted I be up and ready early, even before she woke up. But if I did anything other than sit in the living room and wait patiently for her; if I turned on a cartoon, read a book, or went outside, she'd lose it.

"'What are you doing?' was her favorite question, and she asked it incessantly. I'd shrug and tell her nothing—which happened to be the truth—but that always seemed to be the wrong answer.

"'This isn't nothing,' she would insist. Then, she'd stare at me as if waiting for her child to magically say exactly what she wanted, though I never knew what that was. So, I'd sit quietly until she gave up and walked away, thoroughly disgusted with her daughter.

"All of my actions made her suspicious. Flip phones became available when I turned 16, and I wanted one desperately. She saw them as endlessly dangerous.

"'Who are you going to talk to? Why? When?' Her line of questioning never ended. What could I say? I wanted a phone because I was a teenage girl who hoped to talk to her friends. She used my inability to explain my desire for a phone as proof that I had ulterior motives.

"She accused me of having a secret boyfriend, drug dealer, and secret club I hoped to join. It was all so blown out of proportion that I laughed at her notion of me sneaking off to some speakeasy to score drugs with a boy. But to her, my laughter proved her suspicions of me to be true.

"To my complete shock, she surprised me with a phone one day. I remember staring at the box and not opening it, confident a poisonous snake or horrible trap hid inside. My mom was all smiles that day.

"'Go ahead, honey. Open it!'

"I stared open-mouthed at the phone inside. Mom hadn't bought some cheap, temporary phone; she'd gotten me one of the nicer models with all the bells and whistles. I remember I was one of the first kids at school to have decent games on my phone with a full-color screen.

"Despite my suspicions, I used the phone, and for a few days, it was heaven. Finally, I could talk to friends without Mom looking over my shoulder and questioning every word I said. One of my friends was called Marty in my phone contacts, (she was a huge *Back to the Future* fan), and she texted me constantly.

"One day, mom cornered me with a dark look on her face. 'Who's Marty?'

"'Huh?'

"Her question made my heart pound. I'd never mentioned Marty by her nickname to my mom. I always called her Shelly, which was her real name, to adults. How had Mom figured out her other name?

"Mom held out her hand with a hard, angry gesture. 'Give me your phone.'

"I did, but I still had no idea what the problem could be. She smirked at the screen as she scrolled through my contacts, then called the one labeled Marty.

"'Hi, I'm calling for Marty.' She said it with what was meant to be an exaggerated version of my voice. I heard Shelley on the other end, then Mom responded, 'Don't lie to me. Who's Marty?'

"Shelley didn't have time for my mom's antics, so she hung up. I'm sure she had no intention of making the situation worse, but the dial tone was all the proof Mom needed.

"If you talk to any other boys, I'll kick you out. I'm not letting some slut have her babies in my house.'

"She stormed out and left me staring at my phone. What had Mom just done?

"Later, with the help of some tech savvy friends at school, I figured out my mother had put spyware on my phone. After that, I used it as little as possible and encouraged my friends to text me using a special code I developed. But the thing about teenagers is, if you're too hard to hang around, they drift away.

"To this day, my mom demands detailed reports of how I spend my time, what I'm doing right now, why, and with whom. It's only been after years of therapy that I've finally learned to stand up to her and maintain boundaries. But I still slip into that old exhaustion and give her what she wants when I can't push back anymore."

CHILDREN

The parent gaslighter makes me sad because our parents should be our lighthouse in a dark, confusing world. Rather than helping us navigate school, first loves, or new jobs, a narcissist parent only sees their progeny floating further away from home and finding autonomy. To a self-centered mother or father, that's a terrifying prospect.

Unfortunately, the problem can also flow the other way. As parents age and come to rely on their children for support, some sons and daughters take advantage of their parents' needs. I got lucky enough to meet Marcia, a lawyer who specializes in the rights of the elderly.

She takes on cases about elder abuse, which often include the victim's own children, the church, or those charged with keeping them safe.

"It's heartbreaking," she told me. "The true narcissists do everything they can to make their parents look demented or incapable. It doesn't matter if the mother or father in question is lucid, healthy, and fully capable. Their own kids work tirelessly to convince anyone who will listen that they can't drive, can't be left alone, or are slowly losing their marbles.

"I had one case of a son who constantly hid things from his own mother, then shook his head at her as if she were a ridiculous child when she couldn't find anything. One day, she even caught him stowing her wallet in an odd spot, but when she tried to confront him, he threatened to put her in a home. She got so scared that she ended up apologizing to him, even though he was clearly guilty.

"Another woman took her kids to court because they tried to make a big show of how incapable she'd become at their own church. Apparently, the church had a program to help take care of older parishioners, but only those who couldn't clean or cook for themselves anymore. Her kids seemed to think that if she was a recipient of the charity, then it might be easier to take over her estate before she passed.

"Of course, there are endless cases of people who start to abuse their parents physically in order to control their bank accounts, get them out of their houses, keep them dependent, and sometimes all three. It's shocking. The same people who owe these folks everything turn on them seemingly overnight, though it's clear to me that they've had narcissistic tendencies for years."

Ray talked to me about his own kids, two boys, who changed before his eyes. They went from two loving young men to conniving, middle-aged villains.

"I'll never get over it. I thought I had the best family on earth. I searched my memories for proof that the seeds of their behavior were buried somewhere, but honestly, I can't think of what made them do this.

"First, they started coming over all the time and asked about my bills often. 'You're paying your electricity, Dad? Your gas?' I told them yes, the bank automated it all for me. Why did they care? Neither of them lived in my house. A couple of times, I had to shoo them out just to get some peace.

"After their billing tactic didn't work out, they started telling me about all kinds of banking fraud. They told me story after story about people who called elderly residents and tricked them into sending money to people on false pretenses. I told them that I'd educated myself and the community center had a special course about fraud prevention. But they insisted I be very careful.

"One day, as I sat home alone, the phone rang. It was someone claiming they were calling from the bank and that they needed my account information. My money had been compromised. Now, I know better than to give personal information over the phone. So, I did what I learned in my class—I hung up and immediately called the number back. That's a good trick, by the way.

"I called back, and to my shock, someone answered. It was my son! I gave him an *earful*. I honestly thought he was scamming people like me and called me by accident. Maybe he had one of those auto-dialing doodads. He hung up on me, and I got so mad that I shook in my chair. I had to take a long walk to calm down.

"The next day, he walked in the house with his brother, a big smile on his face. I got up close to him, my finger in his face, and said, 'You have anything to say to me?'

"He shrugged and played dumb. 'Gosh, Dad, what's up? Did something happen?'

"I got so mad and torn up inside that I started to cry. That little liar had the nerve to put his arms around me like he felt sorry for me. I pushed him away, and he made this big show of falling down, but even his brother didn't buy it.

"I tried to talk to my oldest about the phone incident, but he seemed doubtful. He kind of gave me this look and said, 'Are you sure, Dad? You're not confused about anything?' Oh, that did it. I told both of them to stay away from me. Then, I called my bank and let them know that I believed my own kids were attempting to steal from me. I didn't know exactly how, but I wanted some kind of protection on my account.

"The woman at the bank made a comment, something about how they'd come to see her and asked what to do if they needed to take over my accounts. That broke my heart. I'd held out hope that it was only my younger son trying to scam me, but both? I felt everything fall down around me.

"I haven't spoken to them in months, and I don't have any intention to make up with them either. It's a terrible thing to suspect your own children. What if I get Alzheimer's? What if I fall? I can only imagine how happy they would be. It's horrible. It really kills you."

It's hard to imagine a parent so horribly abused by their children, but it happens more often than you might think. The National Care Planning Council estimates that one in ten seniors are abused at home, and about 90 percent of those cases go unreported. Older family members are often certain that if they complain about their families, they'll lose access to transportation or their finances.

In the cases of those living with narcissists, they're probably right.

A COWORKER OR BOSS

Workplaces and their predetermined power dynamics create a place ripe with opportunities to gaslight. We like to think that a good job will let us go about our business without concern for others' insecurities, personal problems, or needs to stomp on someone else's self-esteem. Yet, it happens all the time when people from different walks of life come together in an office or creative space.

As we all get hired at different levels, earn promotions, build popularity, or connect with others at work, some colleagues may see the office as a place to wield their power through lies, intimidation, and gaslighting.

Gaslighters at work can tear apart our productivity. If you have to deal with someone working to undermine you constantly or portraying you as negatively as possible, it becomes impossible to do a good job. All your focus and energy gets redirected the wrong way and responsibilities go untended until finally, you are a horrible employee. In the end, your gaslighter wins.

It can be hard to see gaslighting at work for what it is until it's too late. But I have some signs to look out for as you interact with coworkers, supervisors, or a boss.

Be aware of any false reports of missed or incomplete work reported to your boss. If someone above you gives you assignments, write them down on the day you discussed it, so you can have a clear record of what got doled out. Anytime you're accused of not doing something, check your records. Was that truly assigned to you, or is someone working hard to make you look irresponsible?

Keep track of the stuff on your desk, specifically important documents or items necessary to your job. A gaslighter will want you to doubt your own memory and might move things that belong to you. Their goal is to let everyone in the office see you searching for the missing item desperately. Then, they hope, you'll be known as a scatterbrain who can't keep track of your own stuff.

Gaslighters also love to report mistakes that never happened. Not to say everyone at work is perfect, but a gaslighter often exaggerates or lies about who made what error. This can also function as a way to hide their own mistakes from their higher-ups, making themselves feel better about their sloppiness at the office.

Or, you might hear your idea reported as that of your gaslighter's brainstorm. This happens when teams or pairs have to work creatively together and hash out an idea. Even if you have witnesses that can claim an idea came from you, many won't bother to correct the claim that it came from someone else. Rather, they'll consider it a team effort, so who cares? Your gaslighting colleague depends on this; it sets a low standard so they can continue claiming your successes for themselves.

One of the oddest stories of a gaslighter at work came from a teacher. I tend to assume that teachers are benevolent workers with students as their first concern, but my friend Christina told me the truth. Many people get into education for the chance to feel celebrated and make others look stupid.

Christina

"I taught fifth grade for ten years. I loved teaching, but I hated school politics. What disturbed me more than anything was seeing a fellow teacher not only jump into the gossip that floats around every campus, but use it to her advantage.

"One of our elementary teachers—I'll just call her X—had the principal so snowed in that it boggles the mind. She spent every spare moment in our principal's office, telling him how his style of leadership inspired her, how she hoped to be a genius like him one day, blah blah blah. She laid it on so thick that he started to believe everything she told him, even complete lies.

"First, she went after a reading coach she didn't like. The coach dared to tell X where she needed to improve some of her reading lessons, and X let her have it. She ran to the principal, claiming that she couldn't find her wedding ring after recess. We all thought, surely our principal wouldn't fall for such an immature ploy for attention, but he felt so close to X that he took the bait immediately. The ring turned up in the literacy coach's locker, and that was it. He let her go.

"After that, a lot of teachers got scared of X. Who would she attack next? I did everything I could to avoid her. One day, a member of the fifth-grade staff came into my room sobbing. She said she'd heard from X that our team leader hated her and had already posted a job ad to replace her.

"'I just got a great report from her! How could she do this?'

"I encouraged my friend to take a moment to calm down and ask our leader directly if she had plans to replace her. The two of them talked, and sure enough, this was just more lies.

"I tried to let the principal know about this infighting, but he didn't believe me. After all, I hadn't been in his office at every free period gushing over all of his decisions. But X had, and she found out that I wanted to let her principal puppet know the truth, and she lost it.

"She started harassing me every day. All of it was small stuff, designed to make me notice but not necessarily make a scene. She'd find out my class had time reserved in the school kitchen, and she would show up ten minutes earlier with her own kids, encouraging them to spill and smear ingredients around so the cleaning crew had to come and use up our time. If we headed to the garden, she photographed me and sent pictures to my team leader, asking if she wanted the parents to know how much time her teachers wasted.

"The worst part came when I tried to stand up for myself. I had no one on my side. X already had one firing under her belt, and no one wanted to be number two. I had to suck it up and work with her, despite all of her nonsense. Luckily, my team leader didn't listen to anything X said, though the principal defended her for years.

"I wish teachers like X were rare, but they're everywhere. Something about education attracts the pettiest people in the world. It's a shame, but we have to find ways to work around or stand up to these blatant narcissists."

Haddy

"I had a boss whom I'll never forget. I'll call her C. C came on to manage a design firm I'd worked with for a few months. Before she arrived, we had a really nice office culture. We let customers come in throughout the day and chat with us, check on projects, and offer ideas. I loved it.

"Suddenly, my great boss announced that he was leaving, and C arrived to take his place. C had an odd idea of how we worked in the office. One of her first assignments was to go with us to a big trade show where we got to show off our services and mingle a bit with potential clients. She disappeared for a long time, so long that we were packed up and heading out when she finally came back. She was carrying massive shopping bags—she'd gone shopping! I stared at her, openly shocked.

"'You know you were supposed to be here with us, right?'

"She snorted at my comment and made some dismissive, 'Hey, I'm the boss,' comment, then left us again. She didn't even carry out a sign.

"We tried to ignore her and focus on our work, but C wouldn't be shoved to the sidelines. She pulled clients into her office where she showed them pictures of her traveling all over the world, the gold name plate on her desk, and her framed degrees. All of them backed out, desperate to get away from her, but she made a big show of getting their numbers so she could contact them 'personally.' I'm certain she never did any such thing.

"Even her husband would come in to cause havoc. They made quite a pair, let me tell you. He would demand things like one of our light tables or a laptop, and we'd simply tell him that it was all business stuff and he couldn't borrow it. He'd come back at us with, 'My wife is your superior!' And we'd tell him, yeah, exactly. She makes more money than us, so why are you begging for free stuff?

"One day, I watched C blatantly take credit for my colleague's idea. He went to explain it to her, and she immediately assured him she'd already thought of it and started dialing the client before he'd left her office. He felt really hurt. Before C arrived, we'd always been open about giving one another credit and support. Fed up, I went to C's office.

"'C, we need to talk.' I sat down uninvited and started explaining that she couldn't steal ideas. That was not how we did business. The day she had an original idea, she was welcome to announce it. But if she wanted us to be the creative ones, she had to give credit where it was due.

"She looked at me in silence, then narrowed her eyes. 'What do you need, exactly?'

"I told her I needed her to tell that client that my colleague had the creative solution, not her.

"'I don't know what you're talking about. If your little friend out there is telling lies about me, I'll deal with him myself. And I'll remember that you took his side.'

"I called up our regional manager that afternoon, during her three-hour long lunch.

"C didn't last long. About a week after that conversation, she was gone. I found out that she'd claimed a bunch of business expenses for personal stuff while she worked for us and did take a couple of laptops home. For her husband, I guess. She also reported that she worked 45 hours a week, which was another blatant lie.

"I know I got lucky. There are plenty of people working for supposedly creative geniuses who are complete psychopaths, and they've had their bad bosses for years."

ROMANTIC PARTNER

Love can sustain and make us feel connected to others in this world, but in the wrong hands, it's a weapon.

Gaslighters like love because it opens people up and lets out their vulnerabilities. To a narcissist, a person who feels true love and trusts their partner completely is a person deserving of pity. They feel a kind of disgust at this thing they perceive as a weakness, yet they have no qualms about its exploitation.

We covered some of the typical romantic partner tactics that a gaslighter can use in chapter three, but I'll expand a bit here.

A narcissist sees no reason why they shouldn't cheat but never admits to cheating if they're confronted. Instead, they'll insist it's all in their partner's head, no matter the evidence. Cheating often gives itself away with secondary phones, hastily scribbled notes, and sexy texts, but even a clear paper trail won't make a gaslighter admit to any wrongdoing.

Remember, a gaslighter needs someone to tell them that they're worthwhile, and that takes grooming. Someone targeted by a narcissistic gaslighter requires time and effort to shape into the kind of partner they want. They need to woo their new partner with romance, promises, and declarations of love, but they also want this new partner to doubt themselves at every turn. That way, the narcissist is the source of knowledge, confidence, and even fun in the relationship.

So, the relationship itself becomes a building site to keep the victim in a state of constant doubt and confusion. This happens with the tactics we saw earlier, like word salad, denial, lies, and declarations of love paired with insults. The victim has to feel as if they're never quite right, almost on the mark but not quite. That keeps them trying in order to get back to the love they felt from their narcissist partner in the beginning.

Eventually, the relationship devolves into a bizarre cycle of:

- "I hate you and no longer desire you."
- "You can't leave because I don't want anyone else to have you."
- Repeat.

To keep that cycle at full tilt, the abuser keeps their victim away from any friends or family—anyone who might tell the victim that they're in a bad situation. They also work hard to make the victim doubt their own sanity, so that they feel like they're wasting everyone's time with their presence and instability. Who wants to hang around some loser who can't remember anything, doesn't know anything, and has no confidence? Thank goodness they have their partner—the narcissist one, of course—otherwise, they'd be completely alone.

All of this is reinforced with other tactics, like the narcissist keeping their victim broke. They might encourage their partner to quit their job, buy in excess to drain their account, or they might steal their money. Without financial independence, the victim becomes much less likely to leave and more dependent.

The gaslighter will also be sure to get rumors about their partner circulating among any mutual friends, colleagues, and even family. They want anyone who might support the victim to doubt their claims of emotional or physical abuse before they listen or help.

Many narcissists marry their victims to ensure a lifetime of someone to put down, so they can use them to build themselves up. Others stay in long, horrible relationships of endless misery, on both sides in order to keep up their confidence.

Wendy

"When I met my ex-wife, I remember feeling so happy. I was recently out and hadn't had a chance to date many women. My friends took me to a gay bar to celebrate my new life outside of the closet, and there she was, this lithe beauty. She introduced herself, Tea, and I remember thinking, *Why is she talking to me? All of my beautiful friends are here. Maybe we were meant to meet?*

"Tea and I started dating immediately. She had to see me right away, the next day. I mentioned it to a couple of lesbian friends, and no one seemed surprised. 'She wants to be your first love,' they told me. Others said, hey, enjoy it. You're finally dating within your sphere. So, I made plans with Tea immediately.

"I didn't know about love-bombing until after Tea was out of the picture, but now I know that she love-bombed me hard. She would say things like, 'You light up the room,' and 'I've never felt like this before.' Within a month, she proposed, and I said yes.

"It was then that friends started pulling me aside and telling me they'd heard bad things about Tea. One friend begged me to slow down. If Tea really wanted to marry me, she'd understand if I wanted to reschedule.

"'Live together for a while! There's no rush,' she said, eyes pleading with me. I mentioned her comment to Tea, (big mistake), and she scoffed.

"'She's so hot for you. You know that, right?'

"I wish I could say I listened to everyone, but I didn't. I married Tea, and the gaslighting started immediately. Suddenly, all the romance was gone, and she started denying every sentence she said. She'd suggest we go to the farmer's market, then turn on a movie and settle in. I'd ask what happened, and she'd tell me I was too needy, and she couldn't handle it.

"I tried to get that old romance back. God, I tried. I cleaned for her, I worked overtime to earn some extra money to buy her gifts. I hate to think about who I was in that relationship. The day Tea lost her temper and threw a plate at me, I saw her—the *real* her—for the first time. Suddenly I knew I'd dug myself an incredibly deep home. It was time to crawl out.

"I called up some friends and asked them for help. When they agreed to keep me safe, I sobbed in relief. I didn't even recognize Tea by that point. She'd gone from being my soulmate to my enemy. The women I'd cut out of my life took me back, got me into some LGBT-focused therapy, and talked over what happened with me for hours. I had to work out a lot of my internal problems, and I made sure to take all future romances nice and slow. You need to get married in a month? Keep walking."

GASLIGHTING FROM STRANGERS

I hope you have lots of people around you who love and value you at every opportunity. That's the kind of life everyone deserves. However, all that love and care can lower our guard around people whom we don't see regularly, like doctors, authority figures, even politicians.

Here's a quick list of people around us who may use gaslighting in ways we don't see coming.

Doctors

No group of impersonal gaslighters disturbs me quite like medical professionals. To be gaslit by a doctor shakes a patient so deeply that they often deny it ever happened; their brain can't fathom what just happened. No doctor would work to hurt their patients, right?

Gaslighting from a doctor can take the form of denial of your symptoms. You might be accused of exaggerating, lying in an attempt to get meds, or "imagining" the symptoms. This can make a patient wonder if they *did* imagine the situation. After all, doctors spend their entire careers studying bodies and illnesses. If a doctor tells us we're wrong, shouldn't we listen?

That's exactly what the gaslighting medical professional wants. They depend on the sight of their white lab coat and clipboard to make patients doubt their own knowledge of their bodies. The doctor could use this doubt to deny medications, encourage the patient not to waste the doctor's time by getting a second opinion, or that it's the patient's mental—not physical—health that needs treating.

Frank, an interviewee of mine, told me about a dentist who broke his tooth during a root canal.

"It hurt so terribly, I had tears running down my face. I tried to signal to the dentist to please stop. Something had gone wrong. Instead, he pushed the drill down harder into my molar and screamed at me to shut up. Panicked, I looked over at his nurse, and she smirked at me. I left that office in horrible pain.

"I called him up the next day and attempted to tell him over the phone, 'Hey, there's a problem. I need you to look at this tooth again.' He lectured me, asking, 'Who's the doctor, you or me?' I was so shocked that I hung up and started looking for a new dentistry office. I pity whoever goes in to see that guy. He's a nightmare."

Racists

We all know racism does an endless amount of damage, but a lot of racism is gaslighting. When an entire group can be maligned as "wanting attention" or written off as "uneducated," that's gaslighting on a large scale.

Much like a romantic partner wants their victim to be perceived as mentally unwell, people who maintain the narrative that certain groups should be ignored want to keep a negative lens on that group. Don't make friends with them or spend time listening to them because they're crazy!

Unfortunately, a lot of powerful people buy into these false narratives about Latino, Hispanic, Black, Asian, and other historically marginalized communities in order to write off any claims of injustice. Far too many people reinforce this gaslighting, keeping racist attitudes alive and making people internalize it, even for those who know, deep down, that it's not true.

Today, a ton of racism happens online. The use of memes, false statistics, or facts taken out of context have fanned the flames of racism like never before. I spoke to one friend who told me that his own father started posting hateful things about Muslims. Most of them were cartoons about "towel heads" and images of Arabic people armed with massive automatic weapons standing on American flags.

"Want to hear the worst part?" he asked. "We're from Afghanistan! We're the people he's making fun of."

Of course, narcissists aren't interested in facts. If they have a time and place to make a whole group of people feel small and manipulate others' fears, they'll jump. A lot of these online racists are savvy about the kinds of hashtags, photos, and phrases that get the most attention, and they have huge online followings.

It's all done in an attempt to make the narcissist feel big while hoping to make others look small. Unfortunately for the victims of this gaslighting, these gaslighters are often so desperate for that sense of importance that they'll stop at nothing to keep people afraid and angry, even if they themselves only feel hollow inside.

Politicians

I know this comes as no surprise, but we need to call manipulative politicians' lies and deceptions what they are: attempts at gaslighting.

It gets out of control when it's election time and politicians go out stumping. Many take time to make the other candidates look stupid, out of control, or dangerous or that it is only them that can save the nation, whereas the other candidates will destroy it.

CHAPTER SUMMARY

This chapter covered a ton of information. Here are the highlights:

- Gaslighting can come from many different people, including parents, children, and colleagues.
- We can run into gaslighters in the doctor's office or interactions with authority figures.
- Politicians, teachers, and other respected members of the community can twist their power into opportunities to gaslight others.

In the next chapter, we'll see how gaslighting impacts us in the short and long term, and why it's so dangerous.

5

THE IMPACT OF GASLIGHTING

G aslighting may not strike you as severe in terms of abuse; generally, someone gets duped into a bad relationship, but they usually get out, right?

Well, we hope. The cycle of abuse between a narcissist and their victim—the fight for love, indifference and cruelty, spark of hope, then repeat—can feel impossible to break. How does one fight off the promise of love?

Of course, there are ways, but it's not easy. What's more, the damage done during that endless struggle can't be dismissed. Years of gaslighting don't fade away in a couple of weeks the way other breakups might. The mental anguish haunts us for years, sometimes the rest of our lives.

The wonderful Dr. Robin Stern wrote about the four-stage process in her book, *The Gaslight Effect*. Reading it felt horrible—I actually shook as I flipped through the pages on my Kindle. To see my past relationships laid out in such clear, clinical detail disturbed me deeply, but it had a secondary effect. It freed me. I no longer felt alone and unworthy.

Armed with my new knowledge, I felt prepared to face anything my mind, body, and emotional health needed to build up again. It took time, but more than anything, it took understanding.

Let's dive into the four stages of gaslighting's effects and what we can prepare for as we work on driving away toxic love.

DISBELIEF

If you or anyone close to you dated a narcissist, you're familiar with this phenomenon. Many people use the disbelief stage to forgive themselves for not helping a friend or loved one in a bad situation.

"I tried to tell them!" we declare, certain that was all we could do. "They wouldn't listen to a word I said."

This stage happens to anyone in an unhealthy relationship. A victim doesn't see themselves in a bad light. They're a loved adult—that's how they should be defined. If they met a beautiful or handsome new person at work or the bar who wooed them with concert tickets, walks in the park, or great dinners out. There's no logic to the sudden change in tone. A bad person doesn't take the time to demonstrate love, so how could their partner be evil?

The same happens with children of gaslighting parents. Everyone knows parents pay for things that children need and want. They take the kids to school and get things ready for Christmas morning. How could any parent be a villain?

Even in more casual settings, like between a doctor and patient, a gaslit patient won't believe they could be a victim to the doctor's narcissism. After all, a doctor heals and administers medicine. There's no way a doctor could double as an evil individual... right?

Wrong. The narcissist depends on all of these preconceived notions. They want everyone's guards down and no one to suspect their motives or techniques. It's the veneer of love or care that keeps a narcissist safe from any repercussions.

How does this look in practice?

When a narcissist tells their partner that they're a worthless idiot, the partner's brain works hard to deny the possibility that it ever happened. Instead of thinking, *"What a jerk! I need to get out of here right now!"* they get an error message in their brain. It doesn't compute. This is their love, their friend, and the one they trust more than anyone. There's no way they said that!

The victim convinces themselves that they misheard the narcissist, shaking their head at themselves. When did they get so scatterbrained?

When kids are faced with the cruelty of their parents, it's a similar reaction. Maybe a friend from school realizes a narcissist mom crossed a line when she demanded to see her child's journal. In another case, a teacher has an odd reaction when her student mentions something about not being "allowed" to spend too much time outside.

Whatever the context, the child suddenly has to reconcile the fact that other parents don't behave like their mother and there could be a reason for that.

Kids are experts at explaining things away. They might tell themselves, "Well, other kids have lazy parents. My mom cares more than theirs, that's all." Or they might insist that their mom is right to invade their personal space to keep them safe.

Rather than dealing with reality—that they and their mother have an unhealthy, damaging dynamic—they convinced themselves that they're deeply loved. To face any other reality feels too scary, and no child enjoys being afraid of their own mother.

Disbelief rarely leads to a logical conclusion. Rather, it helps maintain the very thing we need to dismantle. It opens the door and pushes victims through to the second phase.

DEFENSE

No one gets more defensive of a bad partner or out-of-line parent more than their victims. Remember that a narcissist works hard to condition and groom their victim to do what they want, and one of their greatest desires is to be defended.

I'm sure my friends recoiled anytime they heard my weak yet passionate arguments in favor of my narcissist ex-girlfriends, all of whom deserved to be left, not loved.

"You don't understand!" I'd tell them. "She has a really stressful job and has barely slept this week."

Things like that made sense to me at the time. Of course, my girl-friend got a bit short with people. She had to be lovely and charming with all her clients non-stop. That would wear down anyone!

In hindsight, I genuinely wonder if the ex in question ever managed to be sweet and charming with a single person. She could be assertive, flirty even, but to imagine anything deeper is laughable. She couldn't put anyone's needs before her own. I'm fairly certain she acted terribly with my friends as a way of training me to keep her safe from outside scrutiny.

Of course, I can't prove this in my own case. However, I can look at the hundreds of testimonies from my research subjects and see, over and over, how often victims stand up for the one hurting them.

It's sad, but we're quick to defend anyone we love, even when they don't deserve it. Often the same people who look to defend others accept the complete lack of defense for their own current state. They accept feeling alone, even when they're in a (supposedly) loving rela-tionship.

In my case, I usually tried to get others to understand my situation. I dated the worst of my narcissists—Kay—in college, and she insisted I work tirelessly to make her happy. I had to buy expensive clothes on my limited budget so she would be proud to parade me around in front of her fellow design majors. Then, I had to change my hair and get a bizarre, asymmetrical haircut she insisted would put me miles ahead of others in terms of style.

I felt insane walking to class, yet the moment a friend of mine raised her eyebrows at my new look, I went on the defensive.

"Hey, this is the latest style," I told her. She held her hands up in surrender.

"I didn't say a word," she said. But I still caught her rolling her eyes the moment before she walked away. I felt terrible. She probably hoped to ask why the change, but I shut her down so fast she never got a chance.

The exchange made me feel even worse throughout the day. When I saw Kay later that afternoon during our usual post-class coffee, she gave me a fleeting glance as I walked up, then went back to her book. I waited for her to say something about how I wore all the clothes she picked out for me, but she had no comment.

Instead, she had something she wanted.

"You should take me out for dinner tonight," she informed me. "I need it."

"Um, I'm kind of broke..." I looked down at my ridiculous outfit again. It consisted of an artfully shredded sweater and pants so tight they pinched my legs when I sat. She sniffed at my money troubles and sighed.

"You know," she said, looking me up and down, "if you can't afford to dress that way, you can just keep it simple."

My jaw fell open. She and her demands that I work on my style were exactly why I'd bought the damn outfit in the first place! I tried to talk to her about our big fight a week before about how slovenly I dressed, but she waved it away.

"I never said that," she said, rolling her eyes the same way my friend in class had earlier that day.

After all that, I still defended Kay to the first person who had the nerve to point out how little money I had after I started dating her. I immediately launched into my usual explanation.

"Hey, she takes me to tons of events! We're always networking! Thanks to her, I'll have an amazing job and tons of high-paying clients after I graduate! I love her!" And on and on.

You can probably guess how things actually went with Kay. She got consistently worse with her demands, and none of my efforts amounted to anything. By the time I left her, my bank account was overdrawn, I had blue hair in a cut I hated, and I'd lost ten pounds from a combination of stress and an inability to afford groceries.

After the dye faded and I found a little bit of work in a lab on campus, I reflected on the whole experience. Everyone around me tried to have a civil, calm conversation with me about Kay. The only one who overreacted and got angry was me—I'd tossed aside their kindness the same way Kay tossed out any evidence that she'd hurt me.

Other victims I spoke with over the years found themselves reflecting on similar situations. One woman remembered how she'd still defended her father after he started a screaming match with another parent on her school campus.

"I told people all kinds of things. He was the victim of an out-of-control mom, had been sick all the previous week, and didn't understand the problem and thought it was over something personal. You name it, I tried it. Anything to avoid admitting I had a dad who made terrible scenes wherever we took him.

"The worst thing was how triumphant he felt after a horrible, dramatic confrontation. He lived for them! But if anyone accused him of starting them? Oh, that was the last time he'd speak to his accuser. No one who confronted him ever got his forgiveness. In his mind, he had the life of a maligned victim. Everyone around him wanted to 'take him down' or humiliate him in some way. He never considered for a second that he might be in a position to stop the nonsense. I could see in his face that he saw this way of living as non-negotiable. He had to have shouting matches constantly, or else people might see him as weak.

"One teacher offered to help me. She pulled me aside one day and asked if perhaps I needed someone to visit my house and talk to my dad about all the fighting. I shook my head no and insisted she leave me alone. I knew better than to mention the conversation to my dad. He'd have returned to my school to get that teacher fired immediately."

This constant fight to defend the people we love, despite their insistence on behaving terribly, will wear us down over the years. Worse, it works its way into our hearts and minds, leading to the next phase: depression.

DEPRESSION

The depression we will be discussing here is clinical depression that is diagnosed by a medical professional or psychologist. It is a rather tragic part of the cycle; the level of emotional imbalance makes it incredibly difficult and often physically painful for the sufferer to do basic tasks, like getting out of bed, cleaning the house, working, or accomplishing anything mentally or physically taxing.

Many people misunderstand how depression manifests in a person. An individual with depression appears pained most of the day, and I can assure they do feel deep, inescapable pain. However, they're not physically injured, so they push through the hurt to keep going, despite the mental sensation dragging their own body around, which usually comes with their own muscles and bones fighting them the whole way.

Depression occurs due to a chemical imbalance in our brains. Worse, depression presents differently in almost everyone who suffers from it. One person might spend hours and hours in bed in a shallow, unsatisfactory sleep, whereas another may feel angry and restless, unable to sleep at all.

The long-term effects of depression can make it impossible for the sufferer to make important decisions. Depression clouds our judgment like a long session of day-drinking. Our brains are no longer our own, and we become too tired and in too much pain to do anything about it.

I want to clarify all of this because depression is the brain's response to several damaging events happening in our lives combined with past problems and mental illness. All of it comes to a head for victims of a gaslighter rather terribly.

After months or years of trying to defend the narcissist, explaining away or ignoring their hateful behavior and insisting that the victim is loved, the victim can fall deep into a depressive state. The constant fight to find the love they feel certain is just under the surface is more than enough to get them deep into a chemical imbalance.

Unfortunately for our victim, that pained, listless feeling only works to keep them in a bad situation. Suffering from depression, exhaustion, and being worn out on every level, she is no longer strong enough to walk away from the person who got her into this messy state. Of course, the narcissist's disgust only increases when they see their partner this way, but what can they do? the victim at this stage is a husk of their former self. Even the strongest of people struggle to work their way out of this kind of situation, and it can take years for them to find the ability to walk out the door.

I don't write all of this to make you feel obligated to run into someone's personal life, grab them, and drag them out kicking and screaming. Rather, I want you to understand the friend who doesn't leave, even when it seems clear to you that they're deep into a horrible situation.

It's easy to look away when someone's in a bad relationship, but we shouldn't shrug off another person's struggle; we should always try to understand it, not only for their sake, but for our own. When we ignore people, we set ourselves up to be ignored in turn. When my friend Carole talked to me about facing my demons and learning to understand why I felt attracted to narcissists, it may have been hard to hear, but it saved my life.

I met a man called Dave whose ex-boyfriend was a horrific narcissist. The man even hit him a few times, only to shrug off the incidents as his way of joking. Dave worked hard to save the relationship. This was his first real boyfriend, and the thought of that relationship failing broke his heart.

"I remember standing there and letting him hit me," Dave said in an interview. "I mean, I didn't even push him away or put my hands in front of my face. He found some old picture of me with a school friend on social media and demanded to know who it was. When I told him, he threw a knife at me from across the kitchen. And I mean he *threw* it end over end like an action movie villain. By some miracle it missed me, but it still stuck right in the wall."

Dave got so scared of his own partner that he fell into an exhaustion. He lost his job as a social media director for a good company because his productivity fell so low. Then, he found he couldn't exercise anymore; it hurt terribly and required buckets of effort. His lack of enthusiasm for his usual trips to the gym was his first red flag—he had a group of workout friends who reached out and suggested that he may have depression. When he visited a doctor, he burst into tears as he spoke about all the details of his relationship.

"I didn't even have the strength to lie about my boyfriend anymore. It felt so good to tell the truth, but it also brought a whole new pain to the surface. I left that doctor's office with a diagnosis of exhaustion and depression, the name of a therapist, and the sensation of having just been hit by a car. I remember rubbing my chest and feeling a kind of deep bruise, the kind a firehose might leave on a person after they'd been blasted by the police.

"All of it felt like my body screaming at me to do something, to make changes. I got home and told my partner what happened, and he let me have it. He hit me hard across the face, but I barely felt it. I was so under the water by then. That's what pushed me out the door; a smack across the face wasn't enough to make me feel something? That sealed it—I was in trouble."

Dave required years of therapy and treatment to deal with his own self-hatred, depression, and internalized homophobia. But that's another book. I mention him because he's a good example of the underlying issues that can drive us into the arms of a gaslighter and keep us there.

SHORT-TERM EFFECTS

People like Dave fall into a group of lucky survivors. He got out before his partner could do any lasting, physical damage. However, Dave still had to deal with the fallout of that relationship for years. He went to a few therapists until he found one he clicked with, and he also went through a couple of antidepressants before he landed on one that got him back to normal. However, that doesn't mean he felt one hundred percent okay by that point.

"I felt like the ghost of the relationship haunted me for a long time," he told me. "There's no way to prepare for the damage someone can do to your psyche, especially someone you love."

Let's break down the different ways leaving a toxic relationship behind can continue to hurt, even when our ex, former friend, or narcissistic parent is out of our lives.

Mental Health

On a lower level, these relationships wound our sense of confidence deeply. It's impossible to look back on how someone treated us and not judge ourselves for putting up with the insults, mockery, pushes, and punches. Why would anyone stay?

This is a dangerous road to go down. Once we start to question our own judgment, plenty of bad thoughts can enter our minds.

"Maybe I deserve it. It could be payback for that one time..."

"I must want to be abused."

"I guess I don't know what a good relationship looks like. Maybe I never will..."

"Perhaps I'll be single forever."

All of this confusion and self-doubt seeps deep into our subconscious, and we will continue to doubt ourselves for years after our gaslighter walks out the door. That makes big decisions, like when to leave a job, where to move, or who to marry beyond our reach. We start to question everything we do, and that's no way to live.

That same life also makes it impossible to be a friend.

Social Life

All of a former victim's doubts, low self-esteem, and certainty that they deserve horrible things in their life makes it impossible for them to get themselves together in time for a social gathering.

We've all met that person—someone who wants desperately to be included, yet they're terrified of their wish being granted. They sit quietly at the edge of the party, looking down at their feet while fun music plays, people try to include them and maybe even flirt with them to make them feel desirable. But two seconds of flirting can prove to be all they can handle. After that, they're suddenly gone, leaving everyone to wonder, "Who was that odd little wallflower who didn't speak with anyone?"

When we lose our social skills, we forget how to navigate the world. The problem can go far beyond parties. We can no longer manage issues at work, as office politics or misunderstandings may be causing palpitations. Rather than face anyone trying to undermine us or who didn't get all the information, we feel like hiding under our desks. All the bad things suddenly feel deserved and unavoidable. This is now our life, no way around it.

That's all perception, of course. But perceptions are hard to shake, particularly when we can point to a former horrible partner and say, "See? I make bad choices. I like abuse. I can't be trusted in any way, shape, or form."

This attitude turns on us in unexpected ways. All of that, "I deserve this," crap running around in our minds can make us feel endlessly grateful to anyone who shows us even the tiniest bit of kindness. I'm sure you remember kindness and charm can work in a gaslighter's favor. The sudden desire to maintain someone else's happiness—but disregard our own—can leave us back where we started: ripe for the picking.

I feel certain you've met someone who lives to make others happy. This is the person who constantly apologizes or the one who can't stop picking up the bill and constantly suggests that everyone stick together. This is the boss who works endlessly to make their employees love them but not so much on their actual job.

People-pleasing can lead to all kinds of bad decisions. We spend money when we need to save, work day and night to make sure we're in so-and-so's good graces, and spend hours lying in bed and staring at the ceiling, positive we're missing out on some great get-together.

LONG-TERM EFFECTS

We covered depression and how a long relationship with a gaslighter can leave us deep in a depressive state. But what about after we leave?

Depression can get kicked off by a loss. For some, it can be a sudden death in the family or loss of a dear friend. A breakup, even one that's good for us, can have the same effect.

After a relationship ends, our lives are changed forever. Now we have ties to someone we no longer see. Our daily routine takes on a different shape. Those musicals your partner despised are suddenly fair game, and it's no big deal if you decide to spend a weekend watching your favorites.

Going out means we might run into someone who hurt us, so many of us hide in our homes for days, even weeks. We have to explain to our friends what happened and wonder if any of them might choose our ex over us. Losing a girlfriend or boyfriend is rough, but there are also often social casualties that piggyback on the breakup.

All of this can leave a narcissist's victim in the throes of depression. That means the victim won't reach out to their social network, exercise, eat well, or do anything else necessary to stay healthy and balanced. Depression requires regular help from a therapist and possibly medication, yet the people who need the most help often feel overwhelmed by the thought of leaving the house, much less walking into a therapist's office and starting to heal.

Chronic stress will haunt the former victim of a gaslighter for years after they've regained their space. Chronic stress can lead to migraines, as it keeps the muscles in our shoulders and upper back tense. It can also wear muscles out, sometimes so badly that they atrophy. That makes any kind of exercise incredibly difficult and makes it much harder to relax.

Stress can also make respiratory issues like asthma much worse. I found one article that referenced sudden asthma attacks for people experiencing the sudden death of a loved one. If a victim of abuse already has lung problems, the long-term stress can make their issues far more serious.

You may know someone with heart problems under doctor's orders to relax and maintain a healthy lifestyle. That's because high levels of stress affect the heart directly and can lead to a heart attack if they're not managed. The circulatory system also hangs onto the inflammation caused by stress, making heart health a real concern.

The list goes on and on. High levels of prolonged stress can keep us from digesting properly, impair our immune system, and even affect the bowels. Stress can sound like a minor concern at first, but high levels over a long time become major health setbacks. Their submissiveness may put them at risk to be another abuser's target.

Some people develop Post-Traumatic Stress Disorder, (PTSD), making it incredibly hard for them to get back to a normal, functioning state. PTSD occurs in anyone involved in or witnessing a traumatic event. It can even happen indirectly. If someone learns about the violent death of a family member they previously believed passed peacefully, they can experience internal trauma.

PTSD manifests differently in each person. It's an emotional memory that triggers a stress response in the body. For someone who was beaten by a parent or partner, certain smells, sounds, or sights can make their old injuries start to ache, despite having healed. Others might break out into a stress rash after smelling a cologne worn by a former, toxic partner.

It's impossible to know how PTSD will appear, but it's also impossible to ignore once it's activated. It can also maintain a presence in a person's body for years after the event itself. It takes intensive treatment and a lot of hard work on the part of the victim to manage.

Aside from PTSD, depression, anxiety, chronic stress, and everything else it brings along with it, a victim of a gaslighting narcissist can also experience a lot of complicated emotions.

Former victims find it incredibly difficult to trust anyone. How can they? Someone who swore up and down that they loved them suddenly became their worst enemy. After that, anyone who shows any interest in them or extends any kindness will suddenly be suspect. Everyone is a possible enemy in disguise.

Alongside suspicion, many former victims feel terrible guilt. One research subject told me that she honestly punished herself for not "living up to her father's expectations."

"Rather than blame him for constantly moving the standards, I blamed myself. Even when I got older and had a better understanding of the sick games he played, I still felt guilty. I felt it because I participated and kept the game going. I always blamed myself."

That guilt made her feel an incredibly low self-esteem and a high self-doubt. She felt unable to choose groceries, be alone in a room, or anything similar. She had to move in with a close friend and ask her to take care of her. Luckily for my subject, her friend agreed and coached her back to a state where she could build up a schedule, eat regularly, and trust herself to try new things. But it was still a long, arduous process because she didn't see herself as a reliable person.

She also found herself feeling endlessly paranoid. She had to get a new phone because she was certain every call was her father in disguise.

"That's exactly the sort of thing he would do—learn to spoof phone numbers and call me, letting me get excited to hear from a friend, then tear me down. I also had to change to a night job because I was certain he'd haunt all my usual places. I have no idea if he ever did these things, and I didn't let myself find out. I just ran."

Paranoia was a common vein that ran through all the experiences I recorded in my studies, but I also felt it. After Kay and I parted ways, I felt scared to shop. I thought of all the stores as her territory, even the little convenience store under the cafeteria. It didn't matter that she wasn't there—I could feel her as I picked up a bag of chips and went to pay for them. I had to keep checking over my shoulder because I was certain I'd just seen her.

I also carried a deep hopelessness for years. I've discussed that feeling with several people and many of my research volunteers. We lose hope that we know how to pick partners, doubt all of our past decisions, and wonder if we'll ever know what to do as we go through life. We believe certain things will go badly for us thanks to our lapse in judgment, not just in partners, but in everything.

Post-Betrayal Syndrome

All of this brings me to another pressing problem: Post-Betrayal Syndrome, (PBS). This is a physical manifestation of the anger, depression, and sense of loss that occurs, even after a toxic relationship comes to an end.

PBS can take many forms. It can keep a former victim from getting a good night's sleep, keep their energy low, and put their emotions on a permanent rollercoaster.

This syndrome is a distant cousin to Post-Traumatic Stress Disorder, or PTSD. What makes PBS different from PTSD is the sense of disbelief one gets from PBS. How could someone who loved me hate me so deeply? How could I stay and subject myself to all that pain despite all my education and awareness? Remember the error message—the brain can't compute bizarre behavior right away, but after some time, it can look back and parse through the details. But that's rarely a neutral process. It can create an inability to focus and a foggy mental state that keeps the victim stumbling through their day.

PBS is heartbreaking on a much deeper level. Once the victim has some distance and can see just how bad their gaslighter treated them, the pain becomes unbearable. They feel dirty; they've let someone into their psyche, where the gaslighter can stomp around and break everything the victim built for themselves. They get scared—what if they come back? What if my next love turns out to be the same kind of person? What then?

On top of this is the punched-in-the-gut feeling we all feel after an intense, negative interaction. This feeling leaves the victim irritable and with depressive thoughts, possibly even feeling abandoned. If our partner can't be there for us, are we worth anything?

Like PTSD, PBS can lead to a kind of emotional flashback, though mental and physical flashbacks also occur. Small triggers like a turn of phrase, a certain song or the sound of tire wheels on gravel can bring back all the pain for someone recovering from toxic love.

You might be wondering if there's any hope for the victims of gaslighting. It can feel hopeless, even if we leave and stand up for ourselves, but I'm here to tell you that it's far from bleak. There are ways to fight back against the gaslighting narcissists of the world.

We just need to know their weaknesses.

CHAPTER SUMMARY

This chapter delved into the deep, internal wounds caused by gaslighting:

- Serious mental illnesses, like PTSD and depression, can be triggered by gaslighters.
- Chronic stress created by a relationship with a narcissist can lead to a number of health problems.
- A unique syndrome, PBS, is caused by toxic love and relationships.

In the next chapter, we'll learn how to fight back against gaslighting and why you should defend yourself.

6

HOW TO FIGHT BACK

B efore I dive into the techniques in this chapter, I want to clarify that one of the worst things we can do with a narcissist of any kind is actively battle against this person. Nothing makes a narcissist happier than the chance to be a true victim. They seem primed to fall to the floor, a dramatic hand to their foreheads, and cry out, "Why?"

I say fight back, but what I actually want you to do is confront the problem. This strategy is beneficial for everyone involved, no matter the level of narcissism involved. It gives the victim a chance to change the story; they're no longer at the mercy of someone else. Now they're in control and can stay that way for as long as they need.

There's also a miniscule chance—and I don't want you to hold out for this—that a narcissist, once confronted with their actions, might start to question themselves. Again, don't expect to see this happen. I've met very few people who have managed to fight down their insecurities and become fully realized, happy people who didn't need to berate everyone around them emotionally to feel better.

One of the saddest stories I've heard of gaslighting was also a terrifying story of domestic abuse and rape. A woman's new boyfriend attacked her in his apartment and strangled her until she passed out, then violated her. By the time she regained consciousness, she felt terrified. She grabbed a champagne bottle in order to defend herself from him attacking her again, but he filmed her with the bottle, insisting he was the victim, not her. Finally, she grabbed her coat and ran out the door.

This story stands out to me for a couple of reasons. First, this victim saw the reality of her situation right away. I'm with a dangerous person and I need to treat this person as a threat. The moment she tried to fight him off with a heavy object, he didn't run. He turned on his phone's camera and filmed her, screaming that she terrified him and already attacked him once. Finally, she got out. She saw in a moment that there would be no breaking up with this guy. It was get out or get killed.

I love that this woman survived and got herself to safety, but I love her more for facing her attacker. Granted, this is an extreme example, but it proves that no matter how toxic the situation, there's always a way to get out.

Your journey might look completely different from hers. Perhaps the person gaslighting you is a family member or parent. We can't always break up with the bad people in our lives, but there is always a way to save ourselves.

Let's take a look at how we can keep ourselves safe and even confront our gaslighter in a way that puts our sanity first and the integrity of our relationship second.

BE HONEST WITH YOURSELF

Use this book as a guide for dealing with a gaslighter in your life. It's not an easy thing to admit, but it's important all the same. I don't want you to get wrapped up in excuses or explain away someone's behavior. Rather, be honest about how you feel and why you feel that way.

Go over the common phrases I listed in chapter 2 and check off which ones you hear regularly from the person you love. No one who loves you should ever speak to you like this—you aren't crazy, and your feelings aren't unreasonable. You feel sad and confused because your love turned on you, and now your brain can't piece together how it happened.

After you come to terms with your situation, take some space for yourself. Go on a trip with some friends, move in with one of them or a neutral roommate, or head over to your parents' place. Put physical space between you and the person hurting you.

Walking away from anyone who adds stress to our lives gives us a new perception of them and ourselves. When we're physically close to someone we love but who hurts us regularly, it can be hard to remember why we got so upset. Attraction can alter our logic and make it hard to stand by our convictions, and lots of narcissists are beautiful people.

My own ex, Kay, seemed to cast a spell over me with a flick of her wavy blonde locks or a quick wink of her eye. All of my logic would vanish, and I'd feel overcome by the need to hold her. She counted on my attraction to keep me from questioning her. However, once I walked away and got some physical space to myself, I could easily see how she played me. That step back did me a world of good.

BALANCE YOUR EMOTIONAL STATE

Remember that getting upset can make it hard to present your side of a situation or make a coherent argument. Your gaslighter wants you to be an emotional wreck so they can maintain their presence as the calm, logical one in the relationship. Don't fall for it! Do whatever you need to keep yourself balanced.

If we're calm, we can face down gaslighting with a powerful, even stance of clarity. We can call it out and demand our feelings be recognized.

What do you need in order to feel calm and steady? If it's regular exercise, get it, no matter what that entails. You can go online and find a plethora of free workouts. All you need is a little space and thirty minutes to sweat and work out your stress.

If time outside helps you even out, find your natural space and visit it whenever you can. Spending time outside is immensely healing and helps us remember that our problems aren't as massive as we might believe.

Meditation brings millions of people into a peaceful state. You can do it any time of day or night. Find a quiet space and sit or lie down without crossing any limbs and focus on your breath. Notice any distracting thoughts, acknowledge them, then let them go. Return your focus to the in and out of your breathing.

That's it, that's all you need to meditate. Five minutes a day can change your life. I know it did for me, and I'm confident that meditation will help you find a healthy mental state too.

Finding our Zen does more than help us stay firm in our convictions. It also brings the truth to light and makes it impossible to deny. It helps us build faith in ourselves, which ups our confidence and maintains our conviction in our decisions. There's no reason for you to question every move you make, but you will if you don't put yourself and your health first.

IN CASE YOU CAN'T LEAVE

If your gaslighter is someone you can't leave, either because you're a minor and dealing with a manipulative parent or the caretaker for someone toying with your mental state, you still have options.

First, find a way to ground yourself. A friend of mine grew up with vicious anxiety attacks and found a way to calm herself down when her emotions skyrocketed.

"I'd look down at my shoes and show myself that I had safe ground to stand on. Then I'd say, 'Today is December 2nd, 30 degrees outside, the current time is 4 p.m....' and so on. It's hard to get emotional about the date and time, so I always started there. Then I'd look at my location. I'd focus on the walls standing straight up, not moving, and think about the firm foundation underneath me. I'd remind myself that my body is strong, I have no debilitating illnesses, and I can walk without help. All of those irrefutable facts came together to help me move out of the attack."

A grounding exercise can be anything. Try holding and looking at a photo of yourself or someone special to you and focus on the details. Or breathe in for a count of four, hold it for four, then exhale for four seconds. You can also try focusing on a plant in your house, a nearby piece of nature, or the sounds of cars driving by.

The objective is to keep yourself present, no matter the situation. Don't let yourself get caught up in a swirl of thoughts and emotions. Remember that that's when you're at your weakest. With the present reality in your hands, you're much stronger and ready to take on whatever situation you have in front of you.

Evidence is another great way to maintain that mindfulness. Keep a diary—a secret one if you like—and write down any odd events that happen with your gaslighter. List the date and time, write out the details, and tell yourself what happened. Don't worry about what your gaslighter might have to say; this is your space, and no one else gets to have an opinion on your notes.

Refer back to this written record whenever your sanity gets called into question. Use this living document as proof that you don't fabricate moments in your relationship. These things happened and there's no denying it.

Another great way to keep a record of what's happening and how is to keep talking to people around you. You might not feel comfortable opening up about your relationship, so find someone you trust and feel confident will listen to you, not judge you. Don't let yourself get cut off socially; every gaslighter depends on you not having a support system. If you push back on that issue and keep in touch with friends and relatives, you'll always have a voice of reason to back you up.

Other pieces of evidence can include photos of anything you might find important. Maybe you're constantly accused of making a mess, yet everything appears clean and organized. Snap a few pictures of the house and keep them for yourself. Show yourself you aren't imagining anything. You cleaned, and you have proof.

Voice memos can also help you keep track of what happened and when. Each voice recording you save to your phone gets an automatic time stamp. You can also record phone calls, though if you hope to use those recordings in a future case, you'll need to check your state's laws. You may have to ask permission to make a recording legal, which defeats the purpose of recording the call.

Any texts, emails, or messages that reinforce a narcissist's negative message can be screenshotted and saved in a file. Make sure you don't put it somewhere where it can be found—label it with a blasé name and tuck it inside a few other files. Again, check your state's laws if you want to use them in any future cases.

FACING YOUR GASLIGHTER

It's time. Time to let the narcissist in your life know that you see them for what they are: an insecure, manipulative person who makes your daily life impossible.

Before you jump into an argument, be ready for any and all reactions. Your narcissist might laugh in your face, deny the evidence, or use it as a chance to play the victim. Your plan of attack is to stay calm, stay honest, and call this behavior out. No more playing along.

Call It Out

To start, you want to let your narcissist know that what they do with you has a name: gaslighting. You see it, and you don't want it anymore.

Many narcissists see a refusal to fight back as a lack of caring. Remember that narcissists will fight tooth and nail for what they want. They will sacrifice friendships, throw colleagues to the wolves, you name it. Your politeness and tendency to look away could signal to a narcissist that you don't see a problem or care enough to deal with the issue.

Let them know you care. Say it out loud.

"Do not gaslight me. It makes me furious when you do that. Admit you did something wrong so we can move forward."

Clear, concise sentences are your friends. Practice and use them whenever you can to shut down any future gaslighting.

When your gaslighter relies on criticism or insults, respond immediately to the technique, not the words.

"It's not productive for us to sit here and criticize each other. I'm ready to talk about this like an adult. When you're ready, you know where to find me." Then get up and walk away. Don't say you're leaving or where you're going; get out the door without apologies.

This is the same technique lots of parents use when kids are out of control. They simply state that the behavior is unacceptable, then turn and leave. Like small children, narcissists crave attention. When your gaslighter sees that their actions only earn them silence and time alone, they'll start to police themselves (at least a little). But this isn't about them—walking away from the vitriol will make you feel better, too. That's what matters.

You can also shut down accusations of fabricated memories. Here's the reality: our brains don't fabricate entire memories. The brain might change the color of a house or swap two people's names, but it won't build the house and create the people for you. Brains don't work that way. Have confidence that what you remember *is* what happened. If your gaslighter throws the "you're insane" argument your way, you can state that.

"I'm not insane. Far from it. I'm a lucid, mentally stable person. And I know for a fact that there's no such thing as a fabricated memory. You can deny the past all you want, but I know what happened."

Hold onto that confidence in your version of events. Tell yourself you have all your marbles whenever you need to hear it. Say kind things to yourself over and over; it helps more than you might believe. It can also reinforce that you won't accept any manipulative behavior. You don't have time for it because you're living your life.

To help you maintain your stand in the argument, here are some phrases that others in similar situations have found helpful:

- "I have heard your point of view many times now, and I still don't agree with it."
- "I'd like to take a break from this conversation."
- "I don't like how much energy I'm putting into proving my perspective, and it would mean a lot to me if you gave me the benefit of the doubt."
- "I get that you're mad. I'm angry, too."
- "I realize you disagree with me, but this is how I see it."
- "I'm not imagining things."
- "Name-calling is hurtful to me. I find it hard to listen to you when you talk like that."
- "My feelings are my feelings; this is how I feel."
- "This is my experience, and these are my emotions."
- "It sounds like you feel strongly about that, but my emotions are valid too."
- "I feel like I'm not being heard, and I need some space."
- "I know what's best for me."
- "This is what I want and what I need right now."
- "I'm making this decision for myself."
- "I'm not responding to that."

- "I want to figure things out for myself."
- "It's hard for me to stay engaged in this conversation; I've already said no several times."
- "I'm finding it difficult to keep discussing this."

Prioritize Self-Care

Remember that all of this is designed to make you—the one on the receiving end of the abuse—feel better. I don't want you to waste time trying to fix your abuser or hanging onto the belief that one day they'll wake up a saint. We can't control others' actions because it's an impossible feat. What we can control is how well we take care of ourselves and how much we value ourselves as people.

Many mistake self-care as self-indulgence, but it doesn't have to be a day at the spa or lounging in the bathtub, (though that might be your idea of Utopia). Rather, take a moment and think about the simple things in life that make you happy.

What is something you could easily do all day without any thought to a reward? For me it's sipping coffee in a cafe and reading a great book while lounging in a soft armchair. For years, I didn't prioritize taking time for myself. It felt selfish and silly. Couldn't I use that time to work or hit the gym?

Yet, when I allow myself a giant cup of coffee, a good book, and a few hours to enjoy them, my whole week gets better. I get more done at work and I feel happier about my accomplishments. My general outlook stays positive and I don't sweat the small stuff. Despite my misgivings about using my free time to be unproductive, it's proven to be the right thing for me.

Remember that taking care of yourself consists of refilling your happiness quota by finding that thing you revel in for hours on end. It doesn't require a salary or an audience; you just love it because you love it.

For example, a good friend of mine makes time to get her skates on and roll around her neighborhood streets like a kid. She knows she's not a graceful skater nor a particularly fast one, but something about the feel of the breeze in her hair and the sun on her shoulders makes all her problems melt away.

Another friend of mine loves walking in the woods. He sometimes has to remind himself to get home, so he doesn't end up in the middle of nowhere when night falls. His wife loves to see him come home—his former stress has vanished, and she swears he has fewer lines in his face.

We need to make space for our partners to find some time for themselves at least once a week, but we also need to do this for ourselves. Remember that no narcissist would hesitate to do what they love for hours on end. Why should you deny yourself?

Good self-care helps improve your mental, emotional, and physical health. If you feel good, you won't stress-eat or worry over small things, and you will have a better handle on emergencies. Self-care does more than help us relax; it gives us the strong foundation we need to build a more resilient and better version of ourselves.

Hobbies can help you begin your self-care routine. If you want your hobby to be something physical, like hiking up a trail or spending time on a yoga mat, make sure you do it with no goals in mind. Do your best to focus on each moment, not how many calories you burned or the number of miles you logged. Instead, pay attention to your internal strength and balance. Notice the quiet around you and try to hold the same calm in your mind.

Other hobbies help the quiet happen as if by accident. Putting together a complex puzzle, sketching something beautiful, or learning a dance quiets our mental noise. You can feel your worries and stress unravel when you put all your attention into these small projects instead of your current romantic or familial drama.

Try to bring other people into your new interest; doing so can keep you motivated and help boost your social life. Whenever your gaslighter tries to discourage you from meeting up with your running friends or your art club, don't respond. Instead, listen to what he's really saying.

"I'm intimidated by the power you're finding in yourself. I've never experienced that, and I'm scared you won't need me anymore."

Chances are, their right. However, you don't have to say that to your narcissist. Rather, keep your interests and self-care to yourself. It's not for anyone else—those things are available to help you and keep you happy.

THINGS TO KEEP IN MIND

First, always remember what drives a narcissist's behavior. Everything behind a narcissist's actions comes from a place of fear. They're afraid they'll be uncovered as a fraud, be alone, don't deserve love, and everyone else is better than them. They've learned to fight that fear by constantly making others feel terrible, but this sham of a life can't last forever, and they can see the end coming.

Eventually, people around the narcissist—even those who love them dearly—start to see through the cracks. The truly adept gaslighters who can toy with emotions better than anyone else might hide longer, but even they get outed as fake and awful.

Remember all of this, because once you start taking care of yourself, standing up to your gaslighter, and putting yourself first, you'll get pushback.

They'll try everything to keep you to themselves and cut you off from your social life or family. They'll try the love bomb again, showering you with the same tenderness you've hoped for all these years. They might threaten you or themselves, say they'll kill themselves or seriously harm themselves if you leave them.

Stay strong. This is the true sign of a gaslighter and narcissist. Someone with a healthy mental state can handle a night alone; they won't be threatened by physical space and quiet. To a narcissist who feeds on the pain of others, this is torture. They see it as a night in which they'll starve while everyone else laughs at their hunger pangs.

Unlike actual starvation, your narcissist won't suffer. Sure, they'll be uncomfortable, but they'll live.

Remember that you won't be happy if you cancel all your plans to sit around and make someone else more secure. You don't get the days you sacrifice to them back; they're gone for good. Don't surrender your time and energy to anyone else. Keep it safe and use it to benefit yourself, even if it means a showdown.

Try stating simply that you have plans you don't want to break. If your narcissist wants to spend time with you, all they have to do is discuss it with you ahead of time, or you can state that it's unfair of them to expect you to give up your night because you wouldn't do that to them. Say it's good to get some oxygen into a relationship because that's what helps keep it fresh. Do anything that will help you feel confident walking out the door.

You might get a sudden submission like, "Fine! Go! I don't care." Take this at face value. Shrug and say, "Great! See you when I get back," then do whatever you want.

Don't focus on whether your actions qualify as right or wrong. Rather, pay attention to how you feel when you're out on your own or with friends. Are you relieved? Breathing deeper? Hang onto those deep breaths and relaxed shoulders. That's how you should feel every day.

To minimize stress and make yourself more independent, separate your money from your gaslighter. This can get messy, but you need financial independence. Remember that many abusers use money—or a lack of money—to keep their victims in a state of dependence. If you make a salary or receive regular payments, keep those funds in an account that only you can access.

Don't loan out your card or make your passwords too obvious. Narcissists don't hesitate to spend a significant other's money. Keep your accounts secure so you can always have a way to fund what you need and pay for what you want.

TIPS FOR DEALING WITH GASLIGHTERS

Having a separate fund to keep yourself financially independent is one of many ways you can help yourself leave a bad situation. Here's a quick list of things to remember to help you manage your emotions and keep yourself safe.

Don't Take Responsibility

Many victims manage to convince themselves that they're the ones causing the problem. Remember—you can only control your own actions; no one else's are your fault. If your gaslighter loses it in public, walks away from yet another job, or hits someone, none of that is on you.

Also, don't make yourself responsible for someone else's anger or outbursts. All adults have access to resources to help them manage their emotions. If someone in your life can't be bothered to grow up, that's not on you.

Don't Sacrifice

Don't sacrifice your free time, personal space, money, and definitely not your happiness. No one ever won an award for suffering. However, plenty of people find their happiness leading them to great friendships, professional success, and enhanced creative expression. Letting someone take that happiness away from you means you'll lose out on all of those opportunities, so don't do it.

Remember—narcissists both want and despise the people who work hard to make them happy. Yours doesn't enjoy your home-cooked food and constant efforts to feed them healthy food, make the home cheerier or make their friends like you. No matter what you do, what they really want is to see you suffer.

That's why a constant state of sacrifice is a death wish. Always settling for less than the best will leave you dried up and lonely with no one on your side.

Put yourself first and watch your life get exponentially better.

Remember Your Truth

Keep that journal of facts and past events and refer to it all you like. Remember that your brain doesn't fabricate entire memories. That means if you remember something, it happened. That's not up for discussion.

Stand on what you know to be true. When your gaslighter sounds confident, that doesn't mean they're automatically right; it means they are certain they can manipulate you and make you feel weak. Hold onto your personal truth and remember that you never have to defend your emotions; your strength will see you through.

Don't Argue on Their Terms

If your gaslighter makes up a few random facts, then tries to belittle you with declarative sentences like, "you never remember anything right," call out what's happening.

"This is gaslighting, and I won't stand for it. If you want to discuss this like adults, I'll listen. Otherwise, we're done here."

Your gaslighter will try to declare some kind of victory or claim that they've won the argument. You never have to accept those statements. When you can see they're based on a faulty premise, you never have to take any of those announcements as true.

Prioritize Your Safety

If, at any moment, you feel you're in danger, get out. Don't pack a bag or announce that you're leaving. Just open the door and go.

Narcissism and constant gaslighting often lead to physical abuse. Don't kid and try to convince yourself that things will change or get better. That's prioritizing someone else over yourself. Like free time and happiness, safety is something you can't get back after you've put it aside. You have to claim and leave with it, no matter what.

Don't Retaliate

In other words, don't play the gaslighter's game. Using their own tactics against them—like throwing confusing word salad in their face or hitting back—won't work in your favor.

A gaslighter loves to fight. They're drawn to it like a beautiful work of art. They want to spend as much time fighting as possible, so don't give in. Your reactions, loss of control, or yelling reinforce all of their statements about your emotional state and lack of mental stability.

Narcissists need friction. Fights turn them on more than anything. They get to play the victim, and can point to past fights years after they happened as proof that you're a disappointment or the aggressor. It lets the worst side of them come to the surface, and they are vindicated in its appearance. After all, you wanted a fight.

Retaliation often leads to violence, which can endanger your life. Prioritize your safety, don't react, and stand on your truth rather than sink to their level.

HOW TO LEAVE

I've thrown around the idea of walking away from a gaslighter, but how can someone really go with their head held high and feel confident they've made the right decision? Remember that our brains can work against us when it comes to toxic relationships. What if this person is our mother or father? What then?

It's hard no matter who it is that deserves to be left behind, but I promise you there's always a way. It's never impossible to walk away from someone, and it doesn't matter how deep a hold they may have on you.

Here's a breakdown of the stages of getting out of this bad relationship and how to start off on your gaslight-free life the right way.

Leave Mentally

Try a quick visualization. Close your eyes and imagine yourself in two years. See what you look like, what you're doing, and who's there with you. What's your home like? How are you physically? Do you have a new look? Have you lost or gained some weight? Are you happy?

Now go back and try to remember—was your narcissist there with you, or were they out of the picture?

If you can't imagine yourself with someone in the next two years, you're not in a good relationship. It's time to start visualizing yourself as a happy single.

I don't want you to replace your gaslighter with someone new. Remember—one bad relationship can inspire us to run into another one. Instead, think of all the great things you could do without a significant other who makes so many demands on you. Think about all the free time and stress-free days you could enjoy and the number of things you could do if you were on your own.

If the gaslighter is a family member, imagine that person miles away. You may not be able to break up with this narcissist, but you can put them at a great distance. See yourself in a new apartment, and maybe even a new state or country. Physical distance makes it much harder to manipulate someone, so find somewhere you can live where you don't see your gaslighter every day. Don't hesitate to get a new phone number or shut down your social media. If you're less available, you're in less of a position to have to deal with insults and painful comments.

Feel Your Feelings

Be aware of how you feel, but don't judge any of your feelings. Allow them to come in and bang around in your heart. Observe how you feel and when. Maybe you wake up feeling hopeful each morning but slowly get beaten down throughout the day. Do you have a long period of your day that's free of gaslighting? How does it feel during those moments?

Don't label any feelings as good, bad, wrong, or right. Feelings exist to give us greater insight into ourselves. However, it doesn't work if we don't listen.

Our emotions also teach us about our triggers. Your triggers are phrases, actions, jokes, or external factors that make you upset, give you knots in your stomach, or make you want to run out of the room. Even things that indirectly remind us of other things that upset us can be triggers. Triggers are essential to learning how to keep ourselves healthy. Everyone deserves a low-stress life, but that means finding a way to live that's as free from our triggers as we can get.

A good friend of mine, Marnie, absolutely detests hearing women described as "crazy" or "insane." I talked to her about this trigger one day and got some insight into how she developed her specific response.

"First," she explained, "it's a catch-all. As soon as any woman does a single thing a man doesn't like, *she's crazy*. And the description normally comes right behind another word—bitch. It's a word I have to hear all the time because I dare to do things like ask for what's mine, have an opinion, or walk onstage to do my standup comedy. You want to hear that you're a crazy bitch non-stop? Become a woman and hit up an open-mic night.

"Second, there's a long history of people labelling women insane or hysterical and treating them terribly. Mental hospitals used to lock up women if they did so much as hesitate to make dinner for a demanding husband or mention they didn't like something. I'm not exaggerating! Society labeled women clinically insane at the first opportunity for decades. 'Hysteria' was considered a physical and mental disorder just a few centuries ago.

"But here's the big one—I had an ex who constantly called my mental health into question. Now, to be fair, he was joking, but the more I told him it wasn't funny, the more he did it! He'd spent his whole life hearing about us *crazy bitches* and how hilarious it was to call them names; he couldn't hear me when I tried to explain it was *not* funny, but hurting my feelings. I had to leave him, which sucked, because it was all fixable."

"And I'm the one who's crazy?"

I hear Marnie, I really do. I also tried to approach past partners and talk out our problems, only to get dismissed by the same person I adored. What's more is that it creates future triggers, making it harder to be around people who upset or tease us, using words that make us emotional.

Remember that those emotions aren't wrong. You're not overreacting or being sensitive; you're listening to yourself and learning what serves you and what you need to leave behind.

Keeping track of your moods can happen in any journal, but journals can be a pain to carry around. If you need some good apps for journaling or tracking changes in your emotions, I have a quick list for you here.

Moodkit—Moodkit asks you how you're feeling, then uses responses based on cognitive behavioral therapy (CBT) to let you know how a therapist might respond to your feelings. It records your changes in a week and month-long chart, so you can assess different periods of your life and figure out when you feel at your best.

Daylio—Similar to Moodkit, Daylio adds a quick diary, easy stats about mental health, responses, and help in changing your lifestyle. Daylio comes in free or paid premium versions.

CBT Thought Diary—This amazing little digital diary can help you track and reduce negative thoughts. If you tend to beat yourself up mentally, you can use this app to build a more positive view of yourself and focus on what makes you grateful and calm.

TherapyBuddy—An awesome app to have when you start or continue therapy sessions. Most of us see a professional once a week or less, so it can be easy to lose track of what we need to discuss. TherapyBuddy gives you a place to track your time out of a session so you can discuss how you felt on a specific day and what happened that could have knocked you out of whack. Not sure what's stressing you out or why exactly you got so upset? TherapyBuddy can help.

RealifeChange—This one goes beyond tracking by coaching you on how to make better choices. If you struggle to take care of yourself, reach for junk food more than you should, or let others treat you badly, this app can turn your weaknesses into strengths. It also comes in free and paid premium versions.

It's Okay to Walk Away

I know many people who, once something goes wrong, dig in their heels and devote themselves to fixing the problem. This can be admirable. We shouldn't give up on kids who struggle in school or refuse to fight for our health. Once in a while, walking away is better than fighting.

How do we know when to walk away, though? It's not always easy. We have to assess the situation. A therapist I saw for years told me the one question to always ask myself is, "Does this disrupt my life?" That's a quick fix to deciding if something is toxic or simply annoying. Remember that an annoying coworker is someone who can't tell a joke, but a toxic one is a person who loves to watch others suffer.

Does your job leave you feeling defeated, micromanaged, or unintelligent? Do you honestly believe no one in their right mind would hire you if you left? Then it's time to go.

When we can't live our lives normally, we have a toxic force biting at our heels. Once you distance yourself, those bites lose their sting. You can recover and move on to something better, but only if you take the first step away.

Keep reminding yourself that staying means disrupting your life. It means committing to a toxic person, not a loving one. It also means you see yourself as someone who does not deserve happiness and love, but you do!

Before you quit and leave your toxic boss behind, talk to friends in your industry. Tell them you're unhappy and want to see if anyone is hiring. Don't gossip about your boss—that puts you in a bad light. Simply mention that you're hoping to go somewhere else.

You can spend your off-hours clicking through job ads anywhere in the world. You don't have to leave the country; rather, use this as a reminder that yours is not the only place to work. There are tons of opportunities out there you might not have even considered.

If you're not dealing with a toxic boss, but more of a narcissist friend or family member, look for opportunities to put distance between that person and yourself. Remember to prioritize your needs over theirs, and you'll start to make better decisions for yourself. It can be hard to call a family member or lifelong friend toxic, but even these relationships can turn on us for the worst. We need to prioritize our own happiness above all. Spend weekends or afternoons away from the person who is emotionally manipulating you and take notes about how you feel when you're far away from them.

Prepare for the Hoover

Whenever a narcissist sees the writing on the wall or gets confronted with their behavior, they may try to bring out the hoover.

If you have a narcissist in your life, you already know this move. Faced with solitude and loneliness, the narcissist suddenly does a 180. All the former insults suddenly turn into lovely praise. Comments like, "you can't do anything right, can you?" become, "I'm so lucky to have you—you're my hero."

It's as if the narcissist suddenly brought out the vacuum and sucked up all that toxicity poisoning you both in an attempt to fix all the problems between you two.

Of course, erasing the problem doesn't fix anything. Exactly the opposite happens, actually; the victim gets a brief respite from the abuse, the narcissist gets to pretend they're truly a good, caring person, and then slowly, both return to their former patterns. After a few days, the narcissist builds up the negative behavior piece by piece, and their victim slowly falls back into depression and a feeling of helplessness. The victim mentions leaving again, and out comes the hoover for another clean up.

The only way to really fix a terribly broken relationship is with intense couple's therapy. I believe that combined with couple's therapy, individual therapy for both parties has to happen too, although that may not be feasible for everyone. And if your partner, family member, or friend isn't open to it, some real, internal work can't happen.

Get Ready for it to Become Worse

After you leave your narcissist, don't expect them to disappear. Exactly the opposite, in fact. Once you've thrown a narcissist's insecurity in their face, you've lit a fire that will quickly burn out of control.

It's often during and immediately after a breakup that abusive behavior becomes more intense. I can see why so many people stay with monstrous partners—if they leave, they take their lives into their hands. Back home where I grew up, one woman went so far as to plan her own funeral after the police wouldn't help her escape her horrifically abusive ex-boyfriend. Unfortunately, those funeral plans came to be—she was murdered in her own home by the man she'd consistently told police officers was dangerous and needed to be in jail.

I don't mean to scare you, but I do want you to be realistic; if your abuse already includes physical attacks, you need to be ready.

Leave when you're alone or can slip out unseen. Don't say anything or make any kind of a scene. Stay away from mutual friends too— gaslighters often use third parties to spy on former partners. You might think you're safe with your ex's casual friend, but they could be the same reason you're in danger.

Block your gaslighter's number or label it "DO NOT ANSWER" or something similar. Remember that even someone who's bad for us can have a pull on us. Seeing that phrase can keep you from having a moment of weakness. Also, ignore any numbers you don't recognize. Your abuser can easily borrow a phone or buy a burner in hopes of tricking you into answering.

If you can, get a new phone and stay with someone your abuser doesn't know. If the gaslighter is familiar with your place of work, alert your colleagues that your situation has changed. You do not want this person approaching you at work or in the parking lot. If you have security guards at work, let them know and give them a picture of the person you want kept away.

Whenever someone asks for details, decline. Discussing it with others can easily open the door to some truly disgusting accusations against you or a disinterest in your situation that could upset you and make it harder to move on. Simply say, "the situation became a threat to my safety." Anything to shut down the conversation and help you feel in control will be good here.

It's a good idea to contact a domestic abuse organization and ask for a safety plan or a safe place to stay. Many will help you find a volunteer with an extra room or offer you housing with the organization. Then, reach out to any support groups or individual counselors who can help you work through the separation, your residual feelings, and resulting fear, exhaustion, or depression. Plan ahead as much as you can, so you can stay three steps ahead of anyone who might come looking for you with the intent of getting you back to your abuser.

ONE MORE THING...

I know it can be incredibly tempting to go back. Many victims eventually return to their abusers despite the dismal state of the relationship. If this happens to you, don't blame yourself. Remember—your mental state is not what it was in the beginning. In fact, you're a different person altogether and will likely never be the idealist partner you were at the start.

Do everything you can to stay away from anyone in your life who actively and intentionally hurts you. Ask friends to encourage you to do things you love. Avoid anyone who slings mud at your old partner or the narcissist—oddly, this can compel you to defend them and even remember the good times.

After you leave, it's essential that you prioritize your self-care. If you can reduce your hours at work or take a sabbatical, do it. You need this time to show yourself what an amazing person you are and that you deserve better. Don't let anyone tell you that it's wrong to be single or away from the person hurting you. That person isn't you. They cannot know what you've been through, nor will they know what's best for you.

Listen to yourself instead. Pay attention to how you feel and why you want to stay away from your gaslighter. I'm guessing you feel better just by imagining it. Now it's time to plan your escape so you can start to heal.

CHAPTER SUMMARY

It's time to take a deep breath. This chapter was intense. Here's what we discussed:

- Distancing yourself from your abuser will happen in stages. Prepare ahead of time.
- Reach out to any local organizations or mental health

professionals for help.

- Prioritize your happiness and make having a stress-free life your goal.

In the next chapter, we will dive deeper into how to recover from the effects of gaslighting.

7

RECOVERING FROM ABUSE

C ongratulations. You did it. You got away from the person hurting you and took a stand for yourself. I am so glad you're out and ready to move on.

I should say now, you can't do this alone. More than anything, people recovering from a damaged sense of self, brow-beaten mentality, and sense of hopelessness need people around them who can lift them up. You might want to avoid any intense competitions, anyone who likes to make biting comments, and family members whom you know won't take your side.

Before we get into all of that, let me back up. First thing's first, make sure you're safe.

VICTIM OR VICTORIOUS

Step one is how you view yourself. When you look in the mirror, do you see a victim? Someone stupid enough to fall for psychological tricks? Or do you see someone strong enough to move on from this trying experience?

If you answered yes to the former, it's extremely important that you focus on rejecting that victim mentality. It won't serve you and will open the door to future abuse, which is exactly what you worked so hard to leave behind.

Yes, you should acknowledge what happened and how bad it felt, but you also have to see how much power and strength it took for you to walk away. Think of all the wonderful opportunities you have in front of you, with no negative comments making you second-guess your choices. You know now that you're not just sane; you're great. You can start your new and wonderful life, but only if you put your past in the right context.

Think about how things went with your narcissist. Try to remember a time when you stayed quiet and didn't stand up for yourself. Picture it as clearly as you can, and maybe write about it in your journal.

Go ahead and get mad at yourself. Yell at that memory of yourself for the stupidity or reluctance to say something. Get it all out. Then, do it all again. This time see how your silence kept you safe. Maybe it diffused the situation or allowed you to go on with your day. You weren't hiding in plain sight; you were surviving.

Looking back with this new lens will help you move onto a better, more confident you. Confidence shuts down abuse faster than anything—take it from me. I fought for my self-esteem, and it drove away any potential bad partners. They hated that I didn't need anyone because I had myself.

It's important to celebrate who you are as a person. Find groups, events, literature, or films that celebrate different aspects of you. For example, you come from a Latin background, read some of the amazing books from south of the border or incredible poetry. Listen to some great music and pick up some Spanish if you haven't already.

The same can happen for your gender. If you identify yourself as female, try checking out a women's group, a fun, female-centered hobby, or a club. You can sign up for a women-only retreat if it's in your budget and spend a week with a group of incredible, powerful women and soak in that female energy.

Another option is to find people your age who are working to make society better or more fun. If you're young, look for friends who pursue creative expression like the arts or fun garage band music. Look for people who volunteer, work with the homeless, or help any marginalized group in need of some extra hands.

When you surround yourself with happy, positive people, something magical takes place. Happiness is much more contagious than misery, and once we get a taste of it, we wonder why we didn't seek it out much sooner.

After my graduation, I went a year with no work. I had to move back home and hide my face from anyone who might recognize me because

I was so embarrassed. Not only had I left school emotionally scarred, but I also had no prospects despite my endless hours of research. I needed something positive in my life.

I found a great local group called the Dirt Clods. They met once a week to volunteer for an afternoon and take on big projects that nonprofits, daycares, or other groups couldn't afford to pay for, like cleaning the gutters or disinfecting toys.

The group made me so much more hopeful. So many people came together with the sole purpose of helping. Afterwards, we all headed to the bar for a round of beers and to hang out. I was deeply sorry to leave the group after I got hired at my first job.

The Dirt Clods showed me that I had nothing to be embarrassed about. Sure, I was an unemployed graduate living at home with no job offers, but I was more than that. I was a nice guy, a friend, and someone who saw the value in reaching out and helping. As long as I put my energy into something positive, I could be proud of myself.

Another important thing to do now is learn how to create and maintain boundaries. Your boundaries will keep you safe for a lifetime, so set them carefully.

Think about the people who lift you up, make you feel like a part of the group, and love to include you. Write a list of all their names. It's a good idea to spend more time with this group—even if you only get together once a month, do something to show them they matter to you.

Then, write a second list of the people who make you feel small or unimportant. It's okay to put family members or even close friends on this list. We often build relationships that we don't really need or that outlive their value. Maybe you had a close friend in high school that you don't feel close to anymore—decide to let that friendship go. You don't need it anymore.

For family, think about how you can optimize short visits so you don't have to spend lots of time at someone's home when you could be doing something better for yourself. If you have a sister who demands a ton of your free time, visualize telling her you need time for yourself, your friends, or your work. You love her, but you can't be at her beck and call.

You might have to make some lame excuses like, "I would love to come, but I'm swamped." People will likely see through them, but don't stress; you don't owe anyone your time. That's yours alone.

You also need to set boundaries about activities and behavior. What's unacceptable to you? Do you hate a certain kind of humor, people who make explicit comments, or horror movies? From now on, you don't waste time with any of it. You say no thank you and go look for something you enjoy. This world is too big and interesting for you to hang out with a crowd you'd happily toss out the window or watch a corpse get mutilated while you long for an early bedtime, if neither of those activities are things you enjoy doing.

Now, to maintain your boundaries, you need people who respect how you feel. If anyone dismisses how you feel or doesn't listen to you when you express a clear distaste for what's happening, that is someone undeserving of your time. If you get called names or accused of being "sensitive" when you stand up for what you want, consider that a stamp of approval for you to walk away.

EDUCATE YOURSELF

It's important that you learn about abusive behavior, how it works, and the warning signs before you dive into any new relationships. If you don't, it will be easy for you to fall into another bad situation while convincing yourself that everything is somehow different than before.

If you learn about the habits of an abusive partner ahead of time, you can dismiss them before you get love-bombed or deep into their mental traps. The sooner you can give them the boot, the better. You don't need any more narcissists in your life.

Here's a quick list of titles to get you started:

1. *When Love Goes Wrong: What to do When You Can't Do Anything Right* by Ann Jones and Susan Schecter
2. *The Verbally Abusive Relationship: How to Recognize It and Respond* by Patricia Evans
3. *Scared to Leave, Afraid to Stay: Paths from Family Violence to Safety* by Barry Goldstein
4. *Should I Stay or Should I Go?* by Lundy Bancroft & JAC Patrissi

5. *No Visible Wounds: Identifying Non-Physical Abuse of Women by Their Men* by Mary Susan Miller Ph.D.

I could easily write a whole volume of great books to check out, but I like these in particular. You can also join online support groups, in-person group therapy, or whatever else helps you get a better understanding of what happened and why. Remember—you survived, and that's amazing. The next step is to thrive.

LOVE YOURSELF

I know so many smart, incredible people who see themselves as completely unimpressive. It boggles me! A friend with three jobs will call herself "lazy" because she needs a day to rest. A dad who consistently plays and communicates with his kids will write off his parenting skills as "the fun one," despite the value he brings to their childhood. And whip-smart women will still second-guess themselves at work on a daily basis.

I had a long talk with a therapist about my guilt around my selfishness. I saw any attempt to avoid buying gifts—even if I was dead broke —or a refusal to give up my time as me being selfish. By that standard, I had selfish people all around me, yet I didn't see them in that light. I asked her about how I could reconcile my guilt with my needs, and she gave me an interesting exercise.

"What if," she said, "you just said to yourself, 'I'm selfish.'" She cocked her head to the side and put her hands on her hips, the perfect representation of that me-first attitude. "Just tell yourself that and see what happens. I want you to be selfish."

It took a long time, but I eventually got to a point where I could acknowledge that, yes, my decision to avoid a family function or go on a date instead of seeing a needy friend could qualify me as selfish, but that was okay. Life isn't a test of service—it's whatever we make it.

Practice Radical Forgiveness

It seems bizarre, but the act of forgiveness can help the victim much more than the perpetrator. To radically forgive means to acknowledge that without forgiving the person who wronged you, you'll be the one stuck in negativity and anger, not your abuser.

This can take time, and that's perfectly fine. Try practicing meditation, journaling about the experience, and even writing angry letters to your abuser and ripping them to shreds. Then, look for the sadness your abuser must carry.

People who hurt others harbor their own pain. They likely grew up with horrible abuse, a bad sense of themselves, and constant negative messages or lack of support from those around them. I'm not making excuses for anyone, but it's important that we see the whole picture.

Now try writing about how sad and hurt your abuser must have felt in order to pile all that pain onto you. If you know something about their past, acknowledge the roots of that pain and how it built up over the years. It may be unclear how your abuser's pain came to fruition, but that only shows how hard they worked to hide their pain from you.

Start to see your abuser as someone bumbling around in the darkness —someone deserving of pity. Are you still angry? If so, give it some time, talk it over with a therapist, or discuss it in group therapy. You can't be angry and forgive at the same time.

Once the anger starts to dissipate, find a way to forgive your abuser, but not to their face. Instead, do it for yourself. Write them a letter, declare your forgiveness out loud, create something that represents how you've let go of the past relationship. Don't get your past abuser's friends or family involved in any way or post it on social media; keep it private. Make your experience centered on you and no one else.

Radical forgiveness helps us cut ties with a past that no longer serves us. If you can snip those ties away from yourself, you can heal much more deeply and focus on loving yourself non-stop.

This practice also makes it so we don't live in the past. Do you know someone who lives in their memories? I haven't met many—they tend to spend a lot of time alone, don't do well professionally, and often don't move out of their childhood homes. To live in the past means to refuse to move forward, like insisting on standing in a sinkhole. Don't do it.

LET GO OF CLOSURE

A big part of radical forgiveness is the realization that we may never have the closure we crave. It's too much to ask of a gaslighter. Remember that narcissists thrive on others needing their approval, and once your narcissist sees you begging for a chance to talk and put things behind you, they'll dig in. They'll make you chase them and then refuse to give you what you want. Don't believe me? I tried it.

My ex Kay circled back into my life long after I'd let go of our past issues. Then, she started dating a friend of mine, and we ended up at the same party.

I caught Kay alone in the kitchen and we made polite small talk. Then, I asked her if maybe we could get together and talk sometime so we could go over what happened. I wanted to understand where we went wrong.

I'll never forget the little smile that creeped across her face. She lifted an eyebrow and cocked her head at me.

"What? You want to pick me apart? You think you're a shrink now?"

"No, I just thought—"

"That's your problem, you know. You think all the time. It's very unattractive. But sure. Call me sometime and I'll tell you all the issues we had. Why not?"

She flicked her business card at me and walked away.

The card hit me in the chest, and I caught it, then stared at it for a long time. After a long moment, I laughed. What had I expected? Kay hadn't changed—she still loved to make people feel small. I mean, she thought my ability to think was unattractive? I didn't need to call her.

I knew what the problem was, and it was Kay. She loved twisting emotions and making others bow down to her. And I wasn't going to do it ever again.

Some events in life will never give us closure, and that's okay. It's often beside the point. It's up to us to learn from our pasts and fumbles. If we don't, then we lose out on an opportunity. If our former partner, friend, or family member isn't open to learning with us, then we need to let that person miss out. They're not our responsibility.

FORGET SHAME

I read a great quote from a successful porn star that stuck with me for years: "You can't shame me if I don't feel ashamed."

Bam. That's it right there. Granted, she referred to her profession, but the sentiment is still universal. Shame doesn't live long if you love yourself to let go of any semblance of your own shame. What do you have to be ashamed of? You didn't abuse anyone. You're a beautiful, strong individual. You need to see that every time you look in the mirror.

Shame can also enhance that dangerous anchor to the past. Loving and seeing yourself as a constant work-in-progress, not a failed adult or partner, can keep you moving forward. Yes, you'll make mistakes, but you'll learn from them. That's the most anyone can do.

REBUILD YOURSELF

Maybe you made some mistakes in your past, and perhaps you missed out on some opportunities or shrugged off something important. It's fine. You know why?

Because you get to rip it up and start again.

Gaslighting breaks us because it makes us rely on others to define ourselves. Once we get out of the cycle, we have the opportunity to define ourselves. Try letting go of anything you thought about yourself. Maybe you thought you could never be in a musical production or paint a picture. Perhaps you believed for years that you weren't the academic sort or could never write a book.

Let go of all those former misconceptions and be curious about yourself. What would happen if you auditioned for some community theater? What if that roller derby team could become your new group of friends? Would it be so terrible to buy some paints and try creating?

Go into each of these situations and open up to the idea of failure, not because I want you to fail, but simply because you should. If you fail, it means you tried something outside of your comfort zone, and that's a good thing! We learn a lot about ourselves when we attempt something unusual.

Also, be ready to discover that it's the new you. You could strap on those skates and find you never want to take them off. You might fall madly in love with a streak of red paint on a canvas. However, if you go in with a negative attitude or preemptively decide that you're going to hate it, then that can never happen.

Again, be open to discovering yourself. You've spent so long letting others decide how you should spend your time and who you should see, and this is finally your chance to taste lots of different experiences and see what you like.

Before we move on to the next section, I want to add a quick note—please, whatever you do, don't try to get revenge on your narcissist. Revenge, like a prank or some kind of attack on your abuser, might be fun to think about, but don't go through with it. Going out of your way to make their life difficult, get them fired, or embarrass them publicly can easily backfire. Also, they'll see it as further proof of your mental instability and point to it as a way to absolve themselves of their gaslighting sins.

Trust me—the best revenge is you finding your own happiness. That makes you a clear victor. Don't give your abuser anymore of your energy or time, even if it's meant to hurt them. Focus on building your new, better life.

RECONNECT

I'm guessing your gaslighter expected you to have a minimal social life, if any. If that was the case, reach out to those friends you miss seeing and figure out if there's any chance for you to reconnect. Apologize for your absence and admit you were wrong for not prioritizing a positive relationship. Don't make excuses; focus on how you can bring these people back into your life.

The same can happen with family. If your gaslighter kept you away from your parents, siblings, or extended family, do whatever you need to do to get them back. Having people who love and value you in your life is the best way to rediscover yourself and move forward. Don't use these relationships to commiserate about the narcissist. Instead, talk about how important they are to you and how you want to spend time with them in the near future.

Try planning a monthly get-together, like a family dinner, a trip to the local bowling alley, or a movie night. Keep it easy and casual, no pressure if someone is busy or sick. Focus on making it fun and available to show everyone how much you value their love.

If a friend doesn't want to accept you back or chooses your narcissist over you, respect that person's choice. It may be that seeing you and your past issues is a trigger for this person, they could be working through some personal issues that have nothing to do with you, or the friendship may simply be over. That's fine. Acknowledge the choice and move on with your life.

If a family member does the same, put some physical distance between that person and yourself. There are no laws that say families have to get along all the time. When other family members mention your absence, explain in simple terms what happened.

"Mom decided that the emotionally abusive partner I had was the right man for me, despite how much he hurt me. That's more than I can deal with right now, so I'm just giving myself and her some space."

Focus on how you feel and what you're doing, not other people. Change the subject as soon as you can to talk about something positive and uplifting, even if it's small.

"Guess what? My neighbor got the cutest little dog!"

These comments redirect a conversation that could otherwise hurt for a long time. Keep your sights on making yourself happy and not rolling around in misery. I promise it will work.

THE ART OF VOLUNTEERING

I mentioned my own volunteering opportunities earlier, and I want to suggest that you donate a little bit of your time as well. Reaching out and helping someone in your community is the polar opposite of how any narcissist would spend their time. I once suggested volunteering to a narcissist, and he immediately shot back that he would never "work for free."

A lot of people misunderstand volunteering. It's simply showing up. It's holding a ladle for a couple of hours or raking some leaves. It's sitting next to someone who wants to hear a story.

Volunteering couldn't be further from working. You get to decide when it happens, most opportunities don't require an interview, and people are extremely relieved when you show up. Your presence becomes a gift for everyone.

Serving a homeless person food or repairing a broken hinge on the door of an old building does something to our mental state. It reminds us that one of the best ways to benefit is to reach out to others. Whenever I volunteer my time, I walk away feeling brand new, like I've shed old skin. No, I didn't make any money or network with anyone, but I did something intangible. I used my time and energy to make the world a little bit better. It's got value that we can't underestimate.

Don't shoot for more than once a month's worth when you first volunteer. Many people make the mistake of signing up for a high-commitment situation and then get stressed out by the amount of time required. Keep it simple. Volunteer for a holiday, and then see what other opportunities work for your schedule and energy level.

It's okay if you feel doubtful about giving someone your time. It can seem odd at first, but try it and reflect on how you felt during and after the experience. I already know you'll be shocked at how great your day will go after you put some TLC into your community.

GRIEVE

Whenever something ends—a life, friendship, or period in our lives—we feel the loss. Humans need to acknowledge death in all its forms; it's how we go on living.

You will feel the loss of your narcissist and former connection, and you must acknowledge it. You may find you cry or feel extreme happiness at odd times. You might get melancholic and feel tempted to spend several days alone. Chocolate or fatty foods could begin to call your name non-stop.

You need to feel all of this to the deepest degree possible. Let the tears flow, splurge on some junk food, run whenever you feel up to it, and live in the euphoria for a moment. The loss of your former relationship is important, but so is the person you used to be before you met your narcissist. You'll never be them again—you can't be, you've come too far. The new you is beautiful and powerful, but the old you deserves a memorial.

Find a way to mourn the former you and the life you left behind. Put out some photos of that time and say a prayer of thanks and goodbye to the image in those photos. Feel free to invite someone to join you or do it alone, whatever feels right to you.

You might scoff at the idea of mourning the life you once had, but I stand by this practice. I've seen a huge difference in someone's pre- and post-ritual. I can see a weight lifted in those who've said goodbye to the person they used to be and accepted their new selves. They gained a new light in their eyes.

Light that flame in yourself with a quick ritual. You'll be glad you did.

FORGIVE YOURSELF

After you've said goodbye, forgiven your abuser, and found new connections with the people you love, you need to forgive yourself. I'm shocked at how few people look inward and think, "I forgive you." Yet, they're all so quick to forgive others, even some whom they would be justified in never forgiving!

Why do we struggle to forgive ourselves? I'm not entirely sure, but I have some theories.

We often make the same mistakes we've seen others make. That realization—that we did the same thing as someone who made us frustrated or exasperated, creates resentment. I had the bad example right in front of me. Couldn't I see it?

Of course we saw it, but we don't see ourselves with the same lens as others. Also, when we see others struggle, we don't feel the same emotions as the other person. We forget that mental states, emotional problems, and personal histories play huge roles in bad decisions.

So, what can we do? To start, we can look at those poorly thought out decisions and recognize what outside factors came into play. What were we feeling at that time? What were we carrying?

I'm willing to guess that if you tied yourself to a person who turned out to be bad for you, you needed love. And I bet you can forgive yourself for needing a basic human connection. You wanted to feel cherished and build something with a partner. That's a good thing. Maybe you chose the wrong person. That's also okay. Either way, it's time to forgive yourself.

Self-forgiveness can take time, and you'll have to start by stating it out loud. Say to yourself, "I made a mistake. I forgive myself," when you get dressed in the morning. Write it on the mirror so you can read it over and over as you get ready to step out. Do a forgiveness meditation. Say it as often as you need for it to sink in. Then practice that forgiveness throughout your day when you make tiny mistakes. Did you bump into someone on the street? Say you're sorry, then tell yourself you're forgiven.

If you find pangs of guilt sneaking into your regular emotional rotation, acknowledge the emotion. My old therapist suggests giving it a name and a form. My old guilt is a grimy old man who stands too close to others on the train and tells gross stories. Whenever I feel guilty, he appears in my mind, picking his nose and snarling at me.

To help me manage that old guilt, I sat down with the old man and had a long talk with him. I asked him about his childhood, listened to his gross tales, and empathized with him. Then, I offered to build him a house.

I imagined a beautiful cabin in my old summer camp, then mentally placed my guilt character inside it. I told him I appreciated everything he did for me growing up, but it no longer served me. Now, to thank him, I wanted to give my guilt a place to retire and get some rest.

It worked! I visited the cabin a few times, but my guilt really did stay in that little spot. It made it easier to manage and helped me let go of my old negative feelings of myself. I continue to struggle, but I feel much better now that I know my guilt worked hard to teach me things and can now spend his days in the mountains.

CREATE NEW RELATIONSHIPS

People often complain that it's impossible to make new friends as an adult, but I find it's more than possible if you adjust your expectations.

When we're kids, friends are people who come to our houses at every opportunity, fill up our birthday parties, and call us constantly. Adults don't have to maintain that level of connection. We have families and jobs that require our time.

Think of an adult friend as someone you see whenever you can, not someone you see constantly. Chat with someone in line for coffee or at your new volunteer gig. Reach out to someone in a support group or group therapy and ask if they want to hang out sometime. Keep it low pressure and remember to temper your expectations. That person might say yes and then forget to follow through, but that's okay! Adults are busy people.

Make yourself available and open to new relationships, and they'll come your way. If you're trying new things and being kind to yourself, you'll build lovely, positive energy around yourself that others will want to be around. Let it happen organically, and you'll reap the rewards.

GIVE IT TIME

Remember that it may take years for you to recover from a severe gaslighting experience. It's important that you give yourself the time you need to get back to a good state. Don't rush the process or recovery. Give yourself as much patience as you need.

Most importantly, avoid rebound relationships. I would recommend not dating for a year, but I'm just following the AA rule of no serious romances until you've been sober for a year. I think a year to ourselves is a great opportunity to see what wonderful people we are on our own. Then, when we are ready for a new partner, we'd have learned that our love is a wonderful gift we're giving, not a rote gesture of handing something over.

Your heart is fragile, precious cargo. Handle it with care.

GET YOURSELF SOME THERAPY

I've mentioned therapy a few times in this book, but I haven't gone into any of the nuances involved with finding a therapist or building a relationship with one.

Therapists are a unique bunch of people. They're meant to make us feel completely at ease and yet challenge us to look at ourselves, our habits, and our true desires. I know tons of people who are terrified to walk into a therapist's office, yet it's clear to me that everyone benefits from a therapy session.

Think of therapy like a visit to the mechanic—even if your car is in perfect shape, you still need to change the oil once in a while. If you skip it, all kinds of gross stuff can build up in your engine, and soon your car won't function at all.

Therapists are similar to mechanics. They clean out our emotional gunk, even for those who don't have any mental issues. Our brains, emotions, and internal lives are dark and complicated. Why not let a professional under the hood so they can take a look?

It's important that you find the best therapist for you. Here're a few things to consider before you sign up for any treatments.

Budget—What can you afford? Is once a week feasible, or can you only pay for one session a month? Take a look at your finances and decide if a private session is something you can swing or if you need a cheaper alternative.

Physical distance—Keep in mind that therapy requires an hour. If you're late or have to leave early, you won't get the most out of a session. If you have your eye on a center or private office, make sure you can actually get there.

Groups vs Private—Private sessions will always cost the most. Are you open to a group session? Many community centers, churches, and advocacy groups offer a chance to gather and talk as a group. But, this also means you won't benefit unless you share. If you go the group route, make it your goal to share some deeply personal stories. Check out the group, make sure you feel safe, and introduce yourself. If you feel welcome and secure, go back and start talking.

Alternatives—In this new, digital age, there are some amazing ways you can get therapy beyond the traditional couch or circle of chairs. Now therapy is available in a text message or video chat. These services charge a monthly fee that's not the same as a private session, but not free either. Check out groups like TalkSpace or BetterHelp to see what your options include.

Once you get going with your new therapy, pay attention to how your sessions make you feel. A good therapist will bring up emotions you didn't realize you had simmering just below the surface. You should feel comfortable admitting personal mistakes, openly crying, yelling, and anything else you need. No therapist should ever judge or encourage you to do something you feel is wrong.

I've heard some interesting stories from different people in my life about strange moments in the therapist's office. Some felt judged, whereas others felt pressured to lose weight or change their appearance, which I find appalling.

The majority, however, loved their therapy sessions. Even when I'm low on money, I make sure I pay for my sessions with my therapist. I've seen her for years and have no plans of stopping. I tend to go into sessions feeling certain I'll have nothing too deep to discuss, only to get there and realize I have a million things to talk about!

Therapy helps us learn more about ourselves and pick apart the why behind our actions. A therapist can also help us reflect on our relationships with others and why they serve or hurt. Mine also encourages me to do things like exercise and eat healthy. She's in great shape herself, so I listen to her.

More than that though, she helps me see that I'm an individual worthy of love. She encouraged me to write this book, and I'm so glad she did! This project made me remember why I love studying human behavior and helping others. I need to thank her, but I'll make sure to thank myself as well for all my hard work.

And thank you for reading. I hope this book helped you see the light and love yourself again. You deserve it.

CHAPTER SUMMARY

What a great chapter! I love reflecting on all the ways we can grow, heal, and learn more about ourselves inside and out.

- Practice radical forgiveness as a means of letting go of the past, then forgive yourself.

- Reconnect with people you love, volunteer your time, and make new friends as you heal.
- Find a great therapist or group therapy that makes you feel welcome and safe.

This chapter marks the end of our book. Please read the following Discussion section for further help on using this book in a club or support group to keep the conversation alive.

FINAL WORDS

I am so flattered you took a chance on this book and gave it your time and attention. I want to help everyone understand gaslighting better and how it works its way into a relationship, turns on the victim, and becomes impossible to escape. If we do get away, we can have amazing lives and loving relationships if we decide to love ourselves like no one else can.

I know that gaslighting can make the recipient believe they're going crazy. I am familiar with that horrible, head-spinning fear that I might be losing my mind and my partner's words may be my last white-knuckle grip on sanity. It's a terrible feeling, and I want to reassure you that anyone who goes through a round of gaslighting feels the same. Gaslighting, more than anything, is designed to make us doubt ourselves.

The other side of that is the never-ending self-doubt. If you can't trust yourself, you start to lean on the narcissist in your life more every day. After all, narcissists are the picture of confidence. Who better to trust?

Sadly, that's exactly what narcissists depend on: that you doubt your own judgment at every turn. It's a horrible way to live and makes us doubt what we like all the way down to the setting on our toaster. Do we really like it lighter? Why not darker? And we continue our day constantly questioning everything.

But what we question the most is the relationship itself. If we've married a narcissist or moved in with one, we start to wonder if this love is truly what love should look and feel like. Should it be this rollercoaster ride of unpredictable emotion, or should it be a calm, canoe ride from one end of a lake to another?

Gaslighting makes us forget the tranquil lake and focus on the screams and laughter of the rollercoaster. We feel silly for looking for an alternative. Surely, this thing that terrifies us deserves our time and attention. It's what we've committed to; we can't possibly throw it away, right?

It gets even more complicated when gaslighters are the parents in a family. Like my own parents, many people grow up with insults, Mom or Dad laughing in their faces and telling them they're not good enough, you name it. Unfortunately, kids experience the damage of gaslighting much deeper than anyone, as it happens when they're much more impressionable. Some parents work their kids so hard that as adults, they believe they have to surrender their freedom and finances by living at home and funding each parent's lifestyle.

Like the gaslit romantic partners, kids whose parents gaslight them regularly no longer trust their own judgment. Statements like, "I want to go to college out of state," or "I'm going to a party," become grounds for endless criticism. The victim walks away thinking, "Are they right? Am I too dumb for college? Did those guys invite me over just to laugh at me?"

Soon, these kids stop making decisions and rely on their parents to decide for them whenever possible.

This leads to extreme isolation for the victim, no matter the relationship. The loss of friends, loved ones, or free time with peers helps the narcissist reinforce their message. That message is that the victim can't manage their own life and needs to give the gaslighter the reins.

Friends or family may help the victim feel empowered or remember that they don't want to hand over control of any kind. So, any positive presence in the victim's life gets the boot.

Ironically, that handover puts the victim's life into a state of chaos. The last thing a narcissist wants is for their victim to feel any semblance of peace. They need their victim constantly questioning their own memories, decisions, and responsibility for any bad moments, mistakes, or accidents. To do that, the gaslighter blames their victim for everything, despite a lack of evidence. Did the electricity go out? Your fault. Did the dogs eat too early, so their food bowls are empty? You must have forgotten to feed them. Are you sad? Don't blame me! You're losing your mind!

You may wonder if the relationship can be saved. I'm sorry to tell you that I have yet to find a couple that worked through narcissism and gaslighting and found their way to a healthy, balanced outcome. It seems the only way to "save" a narcissist is to leave them. Even then, it's unlikely they'll reflect on their actions healthily. Why should they? They're not the crazy one, you are!

In chapter 6, we looked at how to stand up to a gaslighter in a way that doesn't play their game. It requires you to stay calm, state plainly that what they're doing is called gaslighting and you won't stand for it, and to take some physical space whenever you need it. Any attempt to gaslight them back, meet their manipulation in kind, or lash out will only deepen the abuse and could even elevate it to physical attacks.

So no, I'm sorry to say that I'm not here to save your relationship. Rather, I'm here to save you.

I hope this book clarified what gaslighting is and isn't, and why it's important to recognize it when it happens. I want you to be able to call it out right at the beginning and hopefully quickly get away from the person hurting you. I gave you lots of examples so you can walk into a new situation armed with knowledge of what to look out for, like love-bombing.

Other signs include questioning your ability to remember anything, ditching any conversations about the relationship, or quickly changing the subject and refusing to look closer at their actions. A narcissist will ensure you feel confused, lonely, and lost in the relationship. If you struggle to do anything you like, see the people important to you, or eat the foods you like, you're with a narcissist and need to get away.

After you leave, it's essential that you take care of yourself and your mental and emotional health. I covered this more in depth in chapter 7, but the main points are these:

- **Protect yourself**—don't get into any situations where your abuser has access to you, even from a distance. Change your phone number, stay with someone unassociated with them, and alert your coworkers to the situation, so they won't be allowed in your office or place of work. If you have access to security guards where you live or work, give them a picture of your abuser and tell them not to let them in.
- **Focus on healing**—Love and give yourself endless compassion and patience. Keep in mind that it could take a long time for the effects of the abuse to leave your mind and heart.
- **Rebuild yourself**—Reconnect with friends and people you love whom your abuser may have pushed you away from to keep you weak. Explore new hobbies and friendships, volunteer your time, and be curious about who you are as a person. Try new things with an open mind and see what happens.
- **Do the deep work**—Practice some radical forgiveness to let go of the past and see your abuser as pathetic and sad. Grieve and feel the loss of the relationship, then forgive yourself.

- **Find a therapist**—I can't stress enough the importance of finding mental help after a damaging relationship. Find a group, private professional, or online service that can help you rebuild your mental health.

If you can't leave—and I know many of you can't—I encourage you to find a way to put some physical distance between yourself and the narcissist. If you can move in with another family member or good friend, please do. If you can spend less time around this person, maybe by getting involved in after-school programs or tutoring, that's an option, too. Putting space between the two of you will give your mental health a much-needed break. If you're confronted about your avoidance, state simply that it's intentional.

"I don't like the way you gaslight me. I'm spending time away from you to avoid the negative comments."

Don't argue or fight about it. Your narcissist will likely try to start a big argument about your statements. Instead of fighting back, walk out the door. If you're in physical danger, call the police or record the incident with audio or video so you can go get help afterwards.

The moment you can leave, do it. Walk out the door and don't look back. You'll be so glad you put yourself first.

WHAT NOW?

First, I want to say thank you for reading this entire book and ask that you please leave a review on Amazon. Amazon reviews help others find this book and get the advice they need. All you have to do is click the star for a rating, then write a quick sentence about what you thought of the book. It takes less than a minute, but it can make a huge impact on my ability to reach out to others.

Then, take the tools you learned here to move forward and live your amazing new life. Look for the narcissist and gaslighters of the world. Now that you have a clear definition of them, you'll be able to spot them everywhere. Once you see one, you can cross the street and avoid so much as mere eye contact with that person.

You don't have time to waste on toxic people. You need to go and live your beautiful life.

Are you in a therapy group, book club, or crowd that likes to discuss literature? Read on in the Discussion section of this book for more personal testimonies and questions to help spark conversations on the topic of gaslighting, loving a narcissist, and recovery.

DISCUSSION SECTION

The following case studies and questions are designed for use in group therapy, classrooms, or debates. If you use them in your book club or support group, please let me know. I love to hear from my readers.

1. Here's a quote from a victim of a severe gaslighter: "I wished he would hit me." The woman who said it claimed her husband was seen as a pillar of the community, the face of good. She wished for some physical abuse because it would help others see how much he hurt her with his gaslighting. Have you ever felt that way? What signs can we look for in a person to see the damage from gaslighting and emotional abuse?

2. Gaslighting always kicks off with a love bomb. The narcissist showers their future partner with promises of commitment, gifts, and declarations of new, deep emotions. For most of us,

this is too good to resist, and we often don't recognize these situations as dangerous. Imagine you go on a date and get a big, glittery love bomb from the person across the table from you. What signs can you use to confirm that this is an act? What can you say to leave the situation and make it clear that you're not interested?

3. Now imagine a friend of yours just got love-bombed and tells you that they and their date are now an item. You can see in their face that they've been charmed into believing they've met the perfect partner. What can you do to help them see the truth? What can you say if they insist you're wrong?

4. Many narcissists ooze charm. They want everyone to see them as smart, considerate, and beautiful. What famous person can you think of who originally seemed beautiful and ideal to you, only to reveal themselves as ugly and dangerous? How did the revelation happen?

5. Narcissism is most prominent in men, yet plenty of women are narcissists, too. The gaslighting from a woman can hurt a male partner irrevocably, yet men often hesitate to ask for help. What could you say to a male friend in the throes of emotional abuse if one approached you for help? How could you assure him he's not being overly sensitive or overreacting and point out that he's in a dangerous situation? Do you know of any local organizations you could call to get him professional support?

6. Read the following story about my mother, a devoted narcissist, and how she treated me once I became an adult. See if you can find all the stages of gaslighting listed below:

- Love-bombing
- Idealization
- Devaluation
- Lies and exaggeration
- Repetition
- Wearing out the victim
- Escalation
- Discarding Phase
- Attempts to fix the relationship
- Hoovering
- False hope
- Domination and control.

MY STORY

After I graduated from college, I was proud of myself. I felt like I really found myself in school. I solidified my future career—studying human behavior and helping others—and completed a massive research project that my professors adored. Several encouraged me to apply for a graduate degree and become a professor myself, but I wanted to be out in the world and on the front lines of mental health.

To my shock, my mother came to my graduation. She arrived wearing a classy, cream-colored suit and carrying a massive bunch of flowers. When I walked off the stage with my degree, she dramatically handed over the spray of red roses, then planted a big kiss on my cheek. She wiped away a tear and mouthed, "so proud of you," at me, but I'm sure everyone saw it.

I didn't know what to do or say. This was the same woman who originally laughed out loud at the thought of me going to college. She'd insisted I would only drop out, defeated and in debt. Never mind my great grades in high school. Mom felt certain my academic skills had reached their limit. Now? She seemed like a new person. Even the suit looked fresh from the shop.

My friends raised their eyebrows at the flowers. Some were genuinely impressed, but others were confused.

"Is that your mom? I thought you said she was mean and cold."

"No way that's your mom. I can't believe she'd ever be that nice."

Others eyed the flowers with a sad look in their eyes. They could see what a calculated move that presentation really was and wanted me to be careful.

I shook it off. Graduation day wasn't a life sentence. We were all there for a limited amount of time, and then we could go our separate ways. I sat back for the rest of the ceremony and imagined my new life living with my friend Mike in our two-bedroom apartment. We both had high hopes for our futures. I thought about all the books I would write in my new space while Mike walked the nearby trails, protecting wildlife. We'd be unstoppable.

The day I moved into the new place; Mom showed up with a bunch of housewarming gifts.

"Now," she said, "I got you a couch, but before you put it out on the street, you should know that I bought it secondhand. I know how much you hate being spoiled. Oh, and it came with some throw pillows."

Mike's mouth fell open to a perfect little O as he watched several pieces of furniture get carted into the apartment, compliments of my mother. After everything got put in its place, Mom cooked us a big pan of baked macaroni and cheese, (my favorite), and doted on Mike.

"Oh, I love how outdoorsy you are! You must be so strong. Please take my Don out hiking with you. Promise? Oh, you're the best! It will do him so much good." To my horror, she picked up his phone and put in her own number, then made Mike promise to call her if we had any problems. He nodded and seemed happy to pass on his own number.

Had Mom changed? Was she finally the balanced, happy person I'd always prayed she'd become?

Mom started calling me or Mike whenever she got in the mood. The calls went fine at first, and I felt a strange connection to my mother that I'd never felt before. It was nice. I finally felt like I had a mom, not an enemy.

Then, she invited us out to dinner. She knew we were both struggling to find work and surviving on instant soup, so we jumped at the chance to eat dinner.

Mom invited us out to a decent place with appetizers and a dessert cart. We drooled at the rich smells and sank into our soft chairs, a big step up from our secondhand living room. Mom got there early, no surprise, yet she seemed annoyed when we arrived on time.

"I've been here for twenty minutes," she sniffed as we sat down.

"You said 7:30," I held up my phone to show her the text inviting us out. "It's 7:31. We're on time."

She narrowed her eyes at me and signaled to the waiter to bring her another Chablis. Mike and I looked over our menus and I did my best to ignore Mom's fingernails drumming on the table—never a good sign.

"I hope this place is alright. I know it's a bit..."

I waited for her to finish, but my gut knew what was coming. It gave a little twist, warning me.

"It's a bit what, Mom?"

"You know, expensive," she said, whispering the word. "You boys brought your wallets, right?"

Mike and I sank in our chairs. "Mom, you invited us. You said you would treat. What happened?"

Mom gave her rich-lady laugh, a kind of "Haw haw haw," that I hated. "Mike, dear," she went on, leaning across the table to put her hand over his, "it seems my son is back in fantasy land. I never offered to pay." She picked up her menu and chuckled to herself.

Again, I held up my phone. "I've got your text message right here. Let's go to dinner. My treat. What happened?"

Right away Mom shut down. She toyed with her glass as a waiter approached to ask for our order.

"We need a minute," Mike told him. Then he tapped my arm. "You know what, there's a hotdog cart around the corner. Let's go."

I shook my head at my mom. I couldn't believe she'd pull something like that with Mike. Me, sure, she did it all the time growing up, but to my friend? I seethed.

"I know how phone-hacking works," Mom said, not looking at me.

"Oh, so I hacked my phone and faked a message from you? Is that what I did?" I slammed my fist into the table. Mike gave me a kick.

"Seriously. Let's just go."

I sighed. I knew he was right. Mom wanted nothing more than a scene. I wasn't about to give it to her. "Lead the way."

As we left, Mom yelled something after us about her own son, "refusing to spend time with his own mother!" I didn't look back.

Mom called me up a few days later. Against my better judgment, I answered. I tried to talk to her about what happened at the restaurant, but she denied it.

"Your imagination, darling! It's really something."

"You realize I have a witness, don't you?" At that, she clenched her jaw so hard I could hear it over the phone.

"I didn't call to fight. I thought maybe you and I might benefit from some family therapy. What do you say?"

"Family therapy?" I looked at the phone as if some odd filter that made horrible mothers nicer had somehow clicked on. It hadn't. I shook my head in disbelief.

"Mom, I know you don't want to go to counseling. Don't pretend."

"Well," she purred into the phone, in full flirt mode. I shuddered. "It just so happens I've already made the appointment. I know you're into that sort of thing. Do you want the details?"

"Only if you're paying."

"This again? Really, Don. Grab a pen."

I jotted down the details, trying hard not to roll my eyes. She didn't think I'd buy this, did she?

The day of our therapy session came, and I got on the train. I stared at all the mothers on the train holding small children and laughing with their kids. I wondered how many of them were in family counseling.

I arrived at the appointment early, so I pulled out my phone to see how my friends were spending their Saturdays. They all looked relaxed and happy. I put my phone away.

To my shock, my mother walked in.

"Well, what a nice surprise! You're early. I'll let them know we're here." She went up to a receptionist and had an exceptionally quiet conversation with the woman behind the desk. She gestured to me and both turned to give me a glance. Again, I got that twist in my stomach.

"Mom," I started when she sat down next to me. "This is family therapy, right? I only see people here by themselves." I nodded to the waiting room, where a collection of young adults sat far away from one another, legs jostling with nerves.

"Well, I asked for family therapy. I can't be responsible for everyone else." She picked up a magazine and flipped the pages with a firm snap. Fine, I'll shut up.

We heard our names and headed in. The hallway was dark and felt too small for the building. What was this place?

The therapist's office put me at ease. It was a standard setup with a couple of armchairs and a couch. The woman seeing us, I'll call her Dr. X, looked warm and greeted us with a big smile.

Dr. X shook my hand. "So," she said, "you're Don. I'm so glad to meet you."

"Um, yes. I'm sorry, what kind of therapist are you?"

"I'm actually more of a specialist. I help people like you figure out what's real and what's not."

My eyes closed and my shoulders fell. I looked at my mom and saw her as the same woman who consistently trapped me as a kid.

"Really, Mom? You promised me family therapy, and this is what I get?"

"You see!" Mom said, oddly triumphant. "I never said anything like that. I'm certain he lives in some kind of fantasy world, making up all kinds of characters and interactions. I'm terrified of what he might do." She put her head down and managed to conjure up a couple of tears.

"You know what, Mom? Let's do this. Let's talk to the therapist."

I sat down across from Dr. X, who at that point looked completely lost, and told her the truth.

My mother suffered from Narcissistic Personality Disorder. She wanted to hear a professional say that I couldn't function in the world so she could get me back home and rebuild our former codependent relationship. As with the restaurant, she'd gotten me there on false pretenses, and now wanted to get Dr. X on her side. I let the doctor know she was free to agree with my mother. I happened to be an adult who knew his rights—I couldn't be locked up unless the state ordered me into a mental hospital.

Dr. X listened to all of this with a poker face. She gave my mother the occasional glance, but didn't ask her any questions. I kept my tone calm and took long, slow breaths as I spoke.

Mom, on the other hand, paced the room and scoffed at every other comment I made. I walked the doctor through all of Mom's standard tricks. I told her about how she constantly lived in denial and worked hard to make me look bad. She'd done it for as long as I could remember. It was why my father no longer spoke to either of us—he didn't want any connection to his former wife. I didn't blame him.

Finally, Dr. X asked me to pause. She looked at Mom and asked her, "And how do you feel, hearing your son say these things?"

Mom's anger was at an all-time high. She actually looked red. She crossed her arms and looked at me, but spoke to Dr. X.

"Well, I just cannot believe that Don, my own son, could make up such lies about me!"

"Why don't you sit down and give us your side of the story?" the doctor offered. But Mom wasn't about to fall for that.

"Oh, you're not getting a penny out of me," Mom informed her. She headed for the door and looked back at me. "You are such a disappointment!" and out she went.

I looked back at Dr. X who blinked in confusion at the space Mom had just vacated. "She knows we've already charged her for the hour, right?"

I nodded. "Yes. It's all a show. I'm happy to stay and speak with you if you'd like."

Dr. X nodded. "I never get to work with NPD patients. Tell me some more stories about your mom."

I leaned back against the couch and unloaded all my baggage about Mom. By the time I left, I felt amazing. Dr. X gave me some job-hunting advice and contacts, one of which led to my first position as a researcher.

Mom didn't talk to me for a year. When she suddenly called after her long absence, I asked her about the therapy incident.

"I'm sorry, dear," she said, "I don't have the foggiest idea what you're talking about."

Finally, I want to encourage you to share your own story. Looking at the different phases of gaslighting; what steps can you pinpoint in your own history?

Listen to others in your group and repeat the exercise with each of them separately. Is it easier to see the phases now?

SOURCES

A Deeper Look Into Gaslighting. (n.d.). The Hotline. https://www.thehotline.org/resources/a-deeper-look-into-gaslighting/

American Psychological Association. (2018, November 1). Americanpsychologyassociation.org. https://www.apa.org/topics/stress-body

Bain, L. (2019, August 14). *What Is a Narcissist? 8 Key Traits of Narcissism Everyone Should Know.* Good Housekeeping. https://www.goodhousekeeping.com/health/a28690119/what-is-a-narcissist/

Barnes, Z. (2018, April 20). *PTSD After Domestic Violence: Women Share Their Stories.* SELF. https://www.self.com/story/ptsd-domestic-violence

Bennett, T. (2019, November 25). *What's the difference between having narcissistic personality disorder (NPD) and being narcissistic?* Counseling and Life Coaching - Find a Counselor. https://thriveworks.com/blog/difference-between-npd-and-being-narcissistic/

Best books on identifying and escaping domestic violence. (n.d.). DomesticShelters.Org. https://www.domesticshelters.org/resources/books/identifying-and-escaping-abuse

Bridges to Recovery. (2020, October 12). *I Was the Victim of Gaslighting: How Treatment Helped Me Heal After a Nervous Breakdown.* https://www.bridgestorecovery.com/blog/i-was-the-victim-of-gaslighting-how-treatment-helped-me-heal-after-a-nervous-breakdown/

Brockway, L. H. (2020, October 26). *24 phrases 'gaslighters' use against you.* PR Daily. https://www.prdaily.com/24-phrases-gaslighters-use-against-you/

Brooks, H. (2020, January 30). *How I Healed from Gaslighting and Found Self-Love After the Abuse.* Tiny Buddha. https://tinybuddha.com/blog/how-i-healed-from-gaslighting-and-found-self-love-after-the-abuse/

de Canonville, C. L. (n.d.). *What Is Gaslighting? | The Effects of Gaslighting on Victims Of Narcissism.* Narcissistic Behavior. https://narcissisticbehavior.net/the-effects-of-gaslighting-in-narcissistic-victim-syndrome/

Dean, M. E. (2018, January 22). *Gaslighting: A Sneaky Kind Of Emotional Abuse | Betterhelp.* BetterHelp. https://www.betterhelp.com/advice/relations/gaslighting-a-sneaky-kind-of-emotional-abuse/

Drumming, N. (2018, January 17). *635: Chip in My Brain.* This American Life. https://www.thisamericanlife.org/635/transcript

Ellyn, L. (2018, December 17). *This is not what gaslighting is. - Laura Ellyn.* Medium. https://medium.com/@voltairine/this-is-not-what-gaslighting-is-3372e1876791#

Gaslighting. (2018, June 13). GoodTherapy.Org Therapy Blog. https://www.goodtherapy.org/blog/psychpedia/gaslighting

Gordon, S. (n.d.). *Understanding the Manipulative Behaviors Toxic People Use to Control.* Verywell Family. https://www.verywellfamily.com/is-someone-gaslighting-you-4147470

Hartwell-Walker, M. E. (2018, November 6). *7 Ways to Extinguish Gaslighting.* World of Psychology. https://psychcentral.com/blog/7-ways-to-extinguish-gaslighting/

Huizen, J. (2020a, July 14). *What is gaslighting?* Medical News Today. https://www.medicalnewstoday.com/articles/gaslighting

InvajyC. (2019, September 9). *Gaslighting : An emotional abuse to burn your sanity.* ThriveGlobal.Com. https://thriveglobal.com/stories/gaslighting-an-emotional-abuse-to-burn-your-sanity/

Lonczak, H. S. (2020a, November 3). *What Is Gaslighting? 20 Techniques to Stop Emotional Abuse.* PositivePsychology.Com. https://

positivepsychology.com/gaslighting-emotional-abuse/

Mahaffy, K. (2020, August 12). *What Is Gaslighting and How Does It Manifest In Parenting? - Mom's Choice Awards.* Mom's Choice Awards. https://www.momschoiceawards.com/blog/what-gaslighting-how-does-manifest-parenting/

Mays, M. (2020, September 3). *The Impact of Gaslighting.* Partner-Hope. https://partnerhope.com/the-impact-of-gaslighting/

McAuliffe, K. (2020, July 24). *Gaslighting at Work: How to Recognize It—And Stop It.* Career Contessa. https://www.careercontessa.com/advice/gaslighting-in-the-office/

Mindfulness: A Skill You Can Use to Stop Gaslighting. (2020, October 28). One Love Foundation. https://www.joinonelove.org/learn/mindfulness-the-surprising-skill-you-can-use-to-stop-gaslighting/

Narcissistic personality disorder - Symptoms and causes. (2017, November 18). Mayo Clinic. https://www.mayoclinic.org/diseases-conditions/narcissistic-personality-disorder/symptoms-causes/syc-20366662

Peisley, T. (2018, October 10). *Is narcissism common? The answer may surprise you.* SANE Australia. https://www.sane.org/information-stories/the-sane-blog/mental-illness/is-narcissism-common-the-answer-may-surprise-you#:%7E:text=Most%2C%20if%20not%20all%2C%20of,men)%20is%20diagnosed%20with%20NPD.

R., S. (2019, August 29). *5 Things that Motivate Narcissists – Psych2Go.* Psych2Go. https://psych2go.net/5-things-that-motivate-narcissists-2/

Ranya Al Husaini (@AlhusainiRanya). (2019, April 14). *The Seven Stages of Gaslighting.* Sail Magazine. https://sailemagazine.com/2019/04/the-seven-stages-of-gaslighting/

Rethink, C. A. (2020, April 23). *Gaslighting: 22 Examples Of This Brutally Manipulative Mindf*ck.* A Conscious Rethink. https://www.aconsciousrethink.com/6766/gaslighting-examples/

Rodríguez, G. S. (2020, November 20). *Gaslighting: How to Recognize it and What to Say When it Happens.* The Psychology Group Fort Lauderdale. https://thepsychologygroup.com/gaslighting-how-to-recognize-it-and-what-to-say-when-it-happens/

Rundle, E. (2020, October 29). *Manipulation Tactics Narcissists Use To Destabilise You.* She Counselling. https://shecounselling.com.au/manipulation-tactics-narcissists-use-to-destabilise-you/

S. (2020, July 12). *20 Diversion Tactics Highly Manipulative Narcissists, Sociopaths And Psychopaths Use To Silence You.* Thought Catalog. https://thoughtcatalog.com/shahida-arabi/2016/06/20-diversion-tactics-highly-manipulative-narcissists-sociopaths-and-psychopaths-use-to-silence-you/

Stern, R. (2019, January 3). *Gaslighting in relationships: How to spot it and shut it down.* Vox. https://www.vox.com/first-person/2018/12/19/18140830/gaslighting-relationships-politics-explained

stilllearning2b. (2019, April 23). *Five Empowering Ways to Recover From Gaslighting.* Lessons From the End of a Marriage. https://

lessonsfromtheendofamarriage.com/2019/04/five-empowering-ways-to-recover-from-gaslighting/

Streep, P. (2017, August 24). *The Narcissist's Playbook: Ten Tactics to Recognize*. Psych Central.Com. https://blogs.psychcentral.com/knotted/2017/08/the-narcissists-playbook-ten-tactics-to-recognize/

Walker, R. (2018, June 25). *Gaslighting: a subtle, insidious, form of manipulation, hidden in the darkness,*. Medium. https://medium.com/@drwalker/gaslighting-a-subtle-form-of-manipulation-hidden-in-the-darkness-b87dc095553f

Weiss, S. (2017, March 6). *7 Signs Your Parents Are Gaslighting You*. Bustle. https://www.bustle.com/p/7-signs-your-parents-are-gaslighting-you-42457

What is Gaslighting? (2020, September 20). The Hotline. https://www.thehotline.org/resources/what-is-gaslighting/

What Is PTSD? (n.d.). Web Starter Kit. https://www.psychiatry.org/patients-families/ptsd/what-is-ptsd

Winegar, J. (2016, August 18). *Perpetrators of Elder Abuse Are Usually Family Members*. LongTermCareLink. https://www.longtermcarelink.net/article-2016-8-18-Perpetrators-of-Elder-Abuse-Are-Usually-Family-Members.htm

Winters, V. (2020, December 9). *How Growing Up With Gaslighting From My Parents Affected Me as an Adult*. The Mighty. https://themighty.com/2018/12/parents-gaslighting-emotional-abuse/

Made in the USA
Middletown, DE
13 April 2022